PRACTICE MAKES PERFECT®

Advanced English Vocabulary Games

PRACTICE MAKES PERFECT®

Advanced English Vocabulary Games

Chris Gunn, Lanternfish ESL

New York Chicago San Francisco Athens London Madrid
Mexico City Milan New Delhi Singapore Sydney Toronto

1 2 3 4 5 6 7 8 9 10 QVS/QVS 1 0 9 8 7 6 5 4

ISBN 978-0-07-184114-6
MHID 0-07-184114-8

Library of Congress Control Number 2014935324

This book is printed on acid-free paper.

Also by Chris Gunn

Easy ESL Crossword Puzzles
Practice Makes Perfect: English Vocabulary Games

Contents

Introduction

This workbook contains a collection of vocabulary puzzles organized into thematic units constructed around lists of important English vocabulary needed to discuss those themes. This vocabulary—about 800 words—is generally at an advanced level and includes words and phrases needed to discuss important issues in the world today such as the economy, the environment, and human conflict. With this book, students can learn or review vocabulary items in a fun and motivating way. Teachers or tutors can supplement their lessons by using these games and puzzles for introducing new vocabulary or for reviewing vocabulary taught in class.

Each unit begins with a *vocabulary workout*, which consists of a definition-matching activity plus other activities such as identifying collocations or labeling a list of terms. The vocabulary workout is meant to serve as a reference for the puzzles at the end of the unit, as many of the answers from the puzzles can be found somewhere in the vocabulary workout. As well, much of the vocabulary is utilized in more than one puzzle, which will reinforce it. However, although there are links between the various puzzles and vocabulary workouts, it is not necessary to use all of them at once, as each puzzle could also serve as a stand-alone item.

Hints for solving the puzzles:

1. **Pay attention to collocations.** Roughly speaking, two words are collocations if they occur frequently together so that the combination of words seems natural, whereas combinations of similar words would seem awkward. For example, you *make friends*, but you usually do not say that you *make girlfriends*. In other words, *make* collocates with the word *friend* but not with the word *girlfriend*. Paying attention to which words collocate will help you supply answers to puzzles or at the very least eliminate some potential answers. To illustrate this point, consider the following clue:

   He was ____ with theft.

   The words *accused*, *blamed*, *charged*, *convicted*, *punished*, and *sentenced* are all potential candidates for answers in that they are all crime-related past participles of verbs. However, of that list of verbs, only *charged* collocates with *with*: People can be *charged* ***with*** a crime, whereas they are *accused* ***of*** a crime, *blamed* ***for*** a crime, *convicted* ***of*** a crime, *punished* ***for*** a crime, and *sentenced* ***for*** a crime. Thus, all of the words in the list can be eliminated except *charged*.

2. **Look for instances of word play.** Many fixed expressions in English become fixed expressions precisely because they contain word play such as alliteration or rhyme. Alliteration is a repetition of sounds (often at the beginning of words). On the other hand, two words rhyme if they have the same sound from the final stressed syllable to the end of the word. The greeting *trick or treat* and the idiom *feast or famine* both contain alliteration. The idioms *brain drain* and *doom and gloom* are examples of rhyme.

3. **Use a pencil.** Just because a word fits a particular blank doesn't mean it is the answer. You have to find a word that will solve the puzzle as a whole. If you are having trouble, go back and review the vocabulary workout. As a last resort, the answers to the puzzles are provided in the back of the book.

4. **Most of all, have fun!** These puzzles are meant to be an entertaining source of vocabulary review.

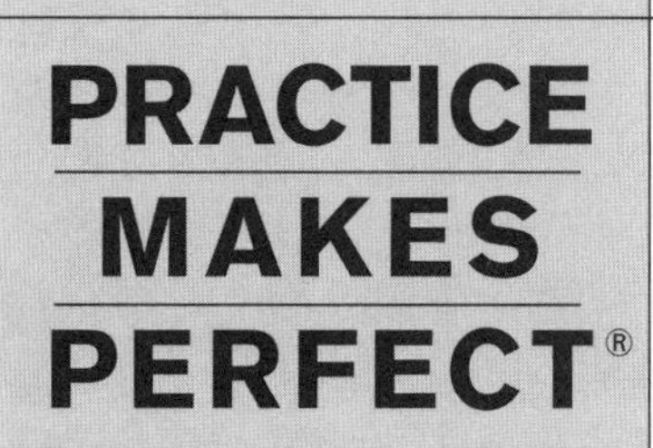

Advanced English Vocabulary Games

Figures of speech

·1·

VOCABULARY

alliteration
hyperbole
metaphor
onomatopoeia
personification
rhyme
sarcasm
simile

PUZZLE
1·1

Definition match-up: Figures of speech *Match the following definitions with words from the vocabulary list. More than one word may fit some of the definitions.*

1. Words that have the same final sound, like *cat/hat*, *cook/book*, or *dish/fish*: ____________
2. A repetition of sounds (usually at the beginning of words), as in *copycat* or *wicked witch*: ____________
3. A comparison of two things using *as* or *like*: ____________
4. A comparison made by saying one thing *is* another thing: ____________
5. An exaggeration or overstatement: ____________
6. Giving human characteristics to something that isn't human: ____________
7. Meaning the opposite of what you actually say in order to be insulting or funny: ____________
8. Words that sound like what they are naming—for example, the *ticktock* of a clock: ____________

PUZZLE

1·2

Identification: Alliteration and rhyme *Many common idioms in English use alliteration or rhyme. Identify whether rhyme or alliteration is being used in the idioms below.*

1. ______________ make or break
2. ______________ sink or swim
3. ______________ doom and gloom
4. ______________ live and learn
5. ______________ burst your bubble
6. ______________ high and dry
7. ______________ a close call
8. ______________ liar, liar, pants on fire
9. ______________ trick or treat
10. ______________ use it or lose it
11. ______________ hustle and bustle
12. ______________ far-fetched
13. ______________ thick as thieves
14. ______________ out and about
15. ______________ wear and tear
16. ______________ brain drain
17. ______________ feast or famine
18. ______________ sky high
19. ______________ through thick and thin
20. ______________ the more the merrier

PUZZLE

1·3

Identification: Hyperbole, metaphor, onomatopoeia, personification, simile, and sarcasm *Read the following sentences and decide what figurative language is being used in the* italic *portion. In some cases, more than one answer is possible.*

1. ______________ Thank you for helping me. *You are an angel*!
2. ______________ The sailors were caught in *an angry wind*.
3. ______________ I'll be back *as quick as lightning*.
4. ______________ The leaves *rustled* in the wind.
5. ______________ You lost the tickets! *Good job*. Now we can't see the movie.
6. ______________ He is the tallest person I've ever met. *He is a giant*.
7. ______________ *Those stains on your shirt are beautiful. They really match your eyes.*
8. ______________ Cherry blossoms fell to the ground *like snowflakes in winter*.
9. ______________ The sun, *curious as to what was happening*, peeked through the clouds.

10. _____________ It's so hot *you could fry eggs on the sidewalk.*

11. _____________ I awoke to the sound of crows *cawing* in the morning.

12. _____________ I'm so hungry *I could eat a horse.*

Fill in the blanks: Figures of speech *Complete the following paragraphs by filling in the blanks using the words provided.*

Alliteration and rhyme

bridges	end	repetition	speech	witch
dandy	poems	rhyme	tear	

Alliteration and _____________ are two very common figures of _____________ in English. Alliteration is a _____________ of sounds, especially at the beginning of words. The expressions *burn your* _____________ and *wicked* _____________ are two examples of alliteration. Rhyme, on the other hand, is when two words have the same sound from the final vowel to the _____________ of the word. The expressions *handy-*_____________ and *wear and* _____________ are two examples of rhymes. You can find rhyme in many songs, _____________, and children's books.

Simile and metaphor

as	feather	giant	saint
comparison	fish	metaphor	

Similes and metaphors are figures of speech that people use to describe something by making a _____________. A simile uses *like* or _____________ to compare two things. The expressions *as light as a* _____________ and *swim like a* _____________ are two examples of similes. A _____________ makes a comparison of two things by saying that one thing *is* another thing. If I say someone is a _____________, I am really saying that the person is very tall. Similarly, if I call someone a _____________, I am really saying that person is a good person.

Hyperbole and sarcasm

accidentally	exaggeration	horse	opposite
actually	good	mean	

Hyperbole and sarcasm are two figures of speech where you say things that you don't really ______________. A hyperbole is an ______________ used to emphasize something. For example, if you say that *you are so hungry you could eat a* ______________, you are saying that you are very hungry. Nobody could ______________ eat a whole horse. Sarcasm, on the other hand, is when you try to be funny or insulting by saying the ______________ of what you mean. When somebody breaks something ______________ and you say, "______________ *job*!" you are being sarcastic.

Personification and onomatopoeia

bird	crow	leaves	nonliving
characteristics	figures	moon	

Personification and onomatopoeia are two more ______________ of speech. Personification is when you give human ______________ to nonhuman things. For example, if you say the ______________ *danced* in the breeze or the ______________ *peeked* into your window one clear night, you are you using personification. ______________ things can't really dance or peek. Onomatopoeia is when a word sounds like what it is trying to represent. For examples, if you say a ______________ *caws* or a ______________ *chirps* you are using onomatopoeia because the words *caw* and *chirp* actually sound like animal sounds.

Idiom puzzle: Figures of speech *All of the idioms that follow are examples of rhymes, alliteration, or simile. Use the symbols below the blanks to help you solve the idioms.*

		HINT
1. A crucial moment:	SINK OR _ _ _ _ ♦ ♠ ◐ 6	Alliteration
2. A crucial moment:	_ _ _ _ OR BREAK ♣ 5 Ω ◈	Rhyme
3. A person who mimics you:	A _ _ _ _ _ _ _ ▲ 17 ● ★ ▲ ♪ ∞	Alliteration
4. Not at home:	OUT AND _ _ _ _ _ 19 ♥ Δ 15 16	Rhyme
5. Sprint fast:	RUN LIKE THE _ _ _ _ ♠ ◐ 9 Σ	Simile
6. Everyone is welcome:	THE MORE THE _ _ _ _ _ _ _ 1 ◈ ▼ ▼ ◐ 23 ▼	Alliteration
7. Educated people leaving a country:	_ _ _ _ _ DRAIN ♥ ▼ 2 ◐ ▣	Rhyme
8. Have a lot to do:	_ _ _ _ AS A BEE ♥ 8 ♦ ★	Simile
9. A chant for choosing:	EINIE, MEENIE, _ _ _ _ _, MO ♣ ◐ 13 25 ◈	Alliteration
10. Hard to Grab:	AS _ _ _ _ _ _ _ _ AS AN EEL ♦ 27 12 ● ● ◈ ▼ ★	Simile
11. No reward without sacrifice:	NO PAIN, NO _ _ _ _ 11 ◐ ▣	Rhyme
12. Good times or bad times:	FEAST OR _ _ _ _ _ _ 18 ♪ ♣ ◐ ▣ ◈	Alliteration
13. Wait a minute:	HOLD YOUR _ _ _ _ _ _ 24 21 ▼ ♦ ◈ ♦	Alliteration
14. Soft to touch:	AS SMOOTH AS _ _ _ _ ♦ ◐ 26 Ω	Simile
15. Get revenge	_ _ _ _ _ _ A SCORE ♦ ◈ 10 ∞ 22 ◈	Alliteration
16. A minor car accident:	A FENDER _ _ _ _ _ _ ♥ 4 ▣ Σ ◈ ▼	Rhyme
17. The whole night:	FROM _ _ _ _ TO DAWN Σ ♦ 3	Alliteration
18. You'd better act quick:	YOU _ _ _ _ _ _, YOU LOSE ♦ ▣ 7 Δ ◈	Rhyme
19. Not rare at all:	AS _ _ _ _ _ _ AS DIRT ▲ Δ 20 ♣ 14 ▣	Simile

PUZZLE
1·6

Code breaker: Alliteration in a proverb

Use the number code in Puzzle 1·5 to solve the proverb.

Overreact to a small problem:

__ __ __ __   __   __ __ __ __ __ __ __ __   __ __ __   __ __   __

1 2 3 4   5   6 7 8 9 10 11 12 13   14 15 16   17 18   19

__ __ __ __ __ __ __ __

20 21 22 23 24 25 26 27

Crossword: Figures of speech

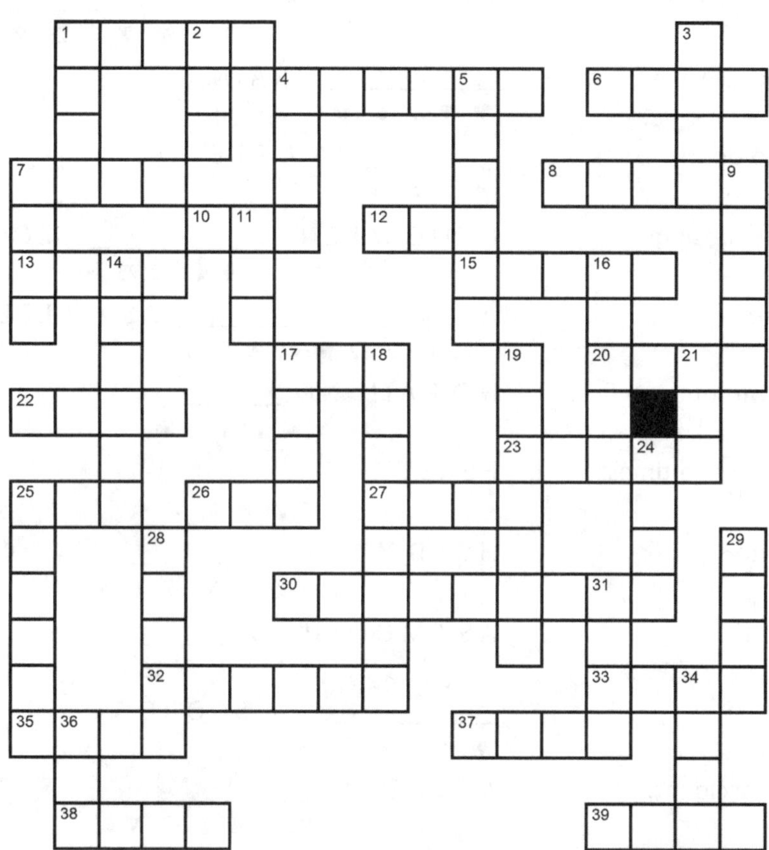

Across

1. (Rhyme) A bakery product that rhymes with *red*.
4. (Alliteration) Bugs and worms: _______ crawlies.
6. (Simile) Quite chilly: As _______ as ice.

Down

1. (Rhyme) A forest animal that rhymes with *there*.
2. (Rhyme) A body part that rhymes with *farm*.
3. (Simile) Squashed: As _______ as a pancake.

Across

7. (Rhyme) A musical instrument that rhymes with *crumb*.
8. (Rhyme) An instrument that rhymes with *toot*.
10. (Simile) Sob a lot: ______ like a baby.
12. (Alliteration) Find ways to save money: ______ corners.
13. (Simile) Simple to do: As ______ as ABC.
15. (Alliteration) Halloween greeting: ______ or treat!
17. (Rhyme) A form of transportation that rhymes with *us*.
20. (Rhyme) A direction that rhymes with *least*.
22. (Simile) Sluggish: As ______ as a snail.
23. (Alliteration) A Christmas treat: ______ cane.
25. (Rhyme) A weather that rhymes with *log*.
26. (Rhyme) A high card that rhymes with *case*.
27. (Alliteration/Simile) Have a lot to do: As ______ as a bee.
30. (Alliteration) A type of cookie: ______ chip.
32. (Simile) Can be found anywhere: As ______ as dirt.
33. (Rhyme) A crop that rhymes with *horn*.
35. (Alliteration) Be careful: ______ before you leap!
37. (Simile) Go straight to the bottom: ______ like a stone.
38. (Alliteration) A doorbell: ______ dong!
39. (Rhyme) A body part that rhymes with *sand*.

Down

4. (Alliteration) A thing that is identical to another thing: A carbon ______.
5. (Simile) Nice to look at: As ______ as a picture.
7. (Rhyme) A forest animal that rhymes with *here*.
9. (Rhyme) A number that rhymes with *great*.
11. (Simile) Sprint: ______ like the wind.
14. (Simile) Has great strength: As ______ as an ox.
16. (Simile) Not dirty at all: As ______ as a whistle.
17. (Rhyme) A color that rhymes with *do*.
18. (Simile) Won't change your mind: As ______ as a mule.
19. (Alliteration) The three Rs: Reduce, reuse, and ______.
21. (Simile) Sneaky: As ______ as a fox.
24. (Alliteration) Very common: A ______ a dozen.
25. (Alliteration) Oil, coal, and gasoline: ______ fuels.
28. (Simile) Very fast: As ______ as a wink.
29. (Alliteration) Money wasted: Money ______ the drain.
31. (Alliteration/onomatopoeia) The sound of a clock: ______ tock.
34. (Rhyme) A type of weather that rhymes with *plane*.
36. (Simile) Ancient: As ______ as the hills.

Academic skills

·2·

VOCABULARY

classify
compare
comprehend
contrast
demonstrate
describe
discuss
estimate
experiment
explain
evaluate
identify
infer
measure
model
observe
paraphrase
predict
prove
record
research
sequence
solve
summarize

PUZZLE 2·1

Definition match-up: Academic skills *Match the following definitions with words from the vocabulary list.*

1. Say what something looks like: ____________
2. Say how two things are alike: ____________
3. Show that something is true: ____________
4. Understand something: ____________
5. Say how something works: ____________
6. Show how something works: ____________
7. Find information: ____________
8. Write information down: ____________
9. Say something in your words: ____________
10. Put things in order: ____________
11. Look at something carefully: ____________
12. See how big something is: ____________
13. Talk about something in depth: ____________
14. Guess what will happen: ____________
15. Say how two things are different: ____________
16. Decide if something is good or not: ____________

17. Sort things into groups: ____________________

18. Find an answer: ____________________

19. Say something in short (usually including only important points): ____________________
____

PUZZLE 2·2

Paraphrasing: Collocating verbs *Rephrase the verbs below by writing a collocating verb in the blank. Choose from among the following verbs:*

do	give	make
find	have	take

1. compare: ____________ a comparison
2. solve: ____________ a solution
3. discuss: ____________ a discussion
4. demonstrate: ____________ a demonstration
5. experiment: ____________ an experiment
6. research: ____________ research
7. predict: ____________ a prediction
8. describe: ____________ a description
9. measure: ____________ a measurement
10. explain: ____________ an explanation

PUZZLE 2·3

Identification: Academic skills in use *Read the following sentences and decide what skills are being used.*

1. ____________ In short, many reptiles are endangered species.
2. ____________ Fish use gills to breathe, whereas reptiles use lungs.
3. ____________ Sharks are a kind of fish.
4. ____________ Chameleons have a long tongue and can change the color of their skin.

5. ______________ Both fish and reptiles lay eggs and have scales on their skin.

6. ______________ In other words, stronger laws are needed to prevent overfishing.

7. ______________ Fish evolved first and then amphibians and finally reptiles.

8. ______________ Many species of reptiles will become extinct in the future.

VOCABULARY

Academic aids

diagram
documentary
glossary
graph
illustration
map
model
table

PUZZLE 2·4

Definition match-up: Academic aids *The nouns in the vocabulary list are things that aid you in learning. Look up any words you don't know. Match the following definitions with the words in the vocabulary list.*

1. A picture that explains something: ______________________
2. A movie about real events: ______________________
3. A collection of difficult words defined: ______________________
4. A picture that shows a relationship: ______________________

PUZZLE

2·5

Crossword: Academic skills

Across

1. _______ a demonstration.
4. Write something down.
6. Say the same thing using different words.
7. A picture that shows the relationship between two things.
8. A film about real events.
9. Solve something: _______ a solution.
10. Discuss something: _______ a discussion.

Down

1. A list of difficult words and explanations found at the back of a book.
2. Say how something works.
3. Check how big something is.
4. Find information.
5. _______ an experiment.
11. Find an answer to a problem.
12. Put something into groups.
13. A picture that shows where things are located.

Across

12. Another word for understand.
15. Show that something is true.
17. _______ a prediction.
18. Talk about something.
19. Put something in order.
21. Say what something looks like.
24. Say what will happen.
26. Determine how good or bad something is.
27. Say something in short.
28. Information organized in columns, or rows with headings.
29. Say how two things are alike.

Down

14. Show how something works.
16. Look at something carefully.
20. Say what you think or feel.
22. Guess how big something is.
23. Say how two things are different.
25. A picture that explains something.

PUZZLE 2·6

Word search: Academic language verbs *Find the following words in the grid.*

E V A L U A T E M H E X P E R I M E N T

R E W H D S P R E D I C T R E C O R D O

E O P E I O E N A U S U M M A R I Z E S

S D C A A L S Q S N C H M E M O R I Z E

E E O O G V O L U D A I D E N T I F Y D

A S M P R E O O R E R L C O M P A R E T

R C P A A C L O E R N S Y D I S C U S S

C R R R M E S A P S R C I Z S O N A E D

H I E A O U C A T T I O E N E I R S T H

O B H P E V O R G A N I Z E C T M O S T

B E E H P R E S E N T N P O N R W E R F

S U N R L G W E M D A F P O O N E W H I

E C D A H R Y O O U C E C E X P L A I N

R A N S U A S E D T O R E S T I M A T E

V C H E A P N G E D E M O N S T R A T E

E E T H E H W O L R L D C L A S S I F Y

analyze compare contrast

classify comprehend create

demonstrate
describe
diagram
discuss
estimate
evaluate
experiment
explain
graph
identify
infer
measure
memorize
model
observe
organize
paraphrase
predict
present
prove
record
research
sequence
solve
summarize
understand

PUZZLE
2·7

Hidden messages *Once you have found all of the words in Puzzle 2•6, the remaining letters form two hidden messages. Uncover the messages and fill in the blanks.*

Quotation 1

__ ___ _____ _ ______ ____ ______

_ ______.

—Victor Hugo

Quotation 2

_________ __ ___ ____ ________

______ _____ ___ ___ ___ __ ______

___ _____.

—Nelson Mandela

Fill in the blanks: Academic skills

Complete the following paragraphs by filling in the blanks using the words provided.

Problem solving

brainstorm	find	outside
creative	ideas	solved

When problems need to be ______________, there are several things you can do to help you ______________ a solution. One thing you can do is ______________, which is thinking up as many ______________ as possible and writing them down whether you think they are good or not. When you do this you should be ______________ and try to think ______________ the box.

Comparison

apples	contrast	make	whereas
both	example	similarities	

When you ______________ a comparison between two things, you look for ______________. For ______________, when you compare frogs and toads you might mention that ______________ animals are born from eggs in water. The opposite of *compare* is ______________. If you contrast frogs and toads you might mention that frogs have smooth, moist skin ______________ toads have bumpy, dry skin. When two things cannot be compared, we say that's like comparing ______________ and oranges.

Classification

animals	characteristics	sort
birds	divided	subgroups

When you classify things, you ______________ them into groups with similar ______________. For example, scientists classify ______________ into two main groups, animals with backbones and animals without backbones. Each of these main groups can be further ______________ into ______________. For example, animals with backbones can be divided into fish, amphibians, reptiles, ______________, and mammals.

Presenting information

columns	graphs	organize	works
diagrams	headings	relationship	

In order to make your arguments clear you need to ______________ your information. Pictures such as ______________ and ______________ can be very useful to help your audience understand. A graph shows a ______________ between two things such as how population changes over time. A diagram is a picture that explains how something ______________. You can also organize your information into a table that consists of rows or _____________ of data with _____________ to let your audience know what the numbers represent.

Making an argument

comprehend	persuade	supporting
examples	summarize	thesis

When you want to _____________ someone, you need to make a convincing argument. You should clearly state your _____________, or main idea, and back it up with good _____________ points. You should also provide concrete _____________ of your supporting points to help your audience _____________ your argument. Finally, you should _____________ your arguments in your conclusion.

Experiments

control	experiment	observe
data	hypothesis	prove

You can test whether or not something is true by doing an _____________. When you do an experiment, you start by making a _____________, which is your prediction of what will happen. You need a _____________ group and an experimental group. You then change one factor in the experimental group and _____________ what happens. The _____________ you gather should help you _____________ or disprove your hypothesis.

Rules and laws

·3·

VOCABULARY

abolish	forbid	obey
allow	impartial	pass
ban	infringe	permit
code	lawful	prohibit
compel	lawsuit	repeal
comply	lax	restrict
compulsory	legal	severe
court case	lenient	strict
enact	liability	transgress
enforce	limit	unbiased
exempt	mandatory	

PUZZLE 3·1

Definition match-up: Rules and laws *Find two words in the vocabulary list for each definition. (More than two may exist.)*

1. Fair, not favoring anyone: ________________ ________________
2. Not allow: ________________ ________________
3. Must be done: ________________ ________________
4. Break a law or rule: ________________ ________________
5. Extreme/harsh: ________________ ________________
6. Make a law: ________________ ________________
7. Follow the law: ________________ ________________
8. Mild/not harsh: ________________ ________________
9. Not a crime: ________________ ________________
10. A dispute settled by a judge: ________________ ________________

PUZZLE
3·2

Collocation match-up: Rules and laws *Match the following words with their collocations.*

act	contempt	due	false	in good	paper
burden	disturb	extenuating	fine	null	smoking

1. ____________ gun
2. ____________ the peace
3. ____________ process
4. ____________ pretenses
5. ____________ of court
6. ____________ of God
7. ____________ print
8. ____________ and void
9. ____________ circumstances
10. ____________ of proof
11. ____________ faith
12. ____________ trail

PUZZLE
3·3

Definition match-up: Rules and laws *Find a collocation pair in Puzzle 3•2 that matches the definitions.*

1. Fair treatment under the law: ____________
2. Strong evidence of a transgression: ____________
3. The responsibility to show that something is true: ____________
4. Uncontrollable situation for which a person cannot be liable: ____________
5. Disrespect toward a judge or the law: ____________
6. Cause trouble: ____________
7. The intentional misrepresentation of facts: ____________
8. Conditions that make a transgression seem less serious: ____________

PUZZLE **3·4**

Labeling: Rules and laws *Attach the following labels to the lists of words that follow.*

Legal responsibility	Things that are mandatory in some countries
Principles of justice	Things that people obey
Severity of punishments	Transgressions of the law

1. laws, regulations, rules ________________
2. paying taxes, military service, telling the truth under oath ________________
3. breach, infraction, violation ________________
4. due process, equality before the law, innocent until proven guilty ________________
5. draconian, lax, strict ________________
6. accountability, fault, liability ________________

PUZZLE **3·5**

Fill in the blanks: Rules and laws *Complete the following paragraphs by filling in the blanks using the words provided.*

Principles of justice

disputes	fundamental	infringed	revenge	treatment
equality	hands	principles	sue	

Modern democracies depend on the court system to settle ____________ among citizens. Citizens who feel their rights have been ____________ upon by others cannot seek ____________ and take the law into their own ____________. Instead, they can ____________ somebody in a court of law. Although different nations have different legal systems, there are some basic ____________ in common. One ____________ principle is the principle of ____________ before the law. This principle states that all citizens receive the same ____________ under the law.

Age of majority

adults	consume	majority	prohibited
allowed	lenient	minors	rights

In many countries, citizens do not receive the full ____________ and responsibilities of citizenship till they become ____________. The age at which citizens are adults under the law is called the age of ____________. Citizens who have not reached this age are called ____________. In many countries, minors are not ____________ to vote or _____________ alcohol. They are also _____________ from serving in the military or holding government office. Also, when minors break the law, they often receive more _____________ penalties than adults do for the same crime.

Citizen responsibilities

legal	military	protect	responsbilities
mandatory	oath	required	voluntary

Good government and a good _____________ system should _____________ the rights of citizens. In turn, citizens have legal _____________ to their government. For example, all over the world paying taxes to the government is _____________. As well, citizens are _____________ to obey the law and tell the truth under _____________. Not all countries place the same demands on citizens, however. In some countries, _____________ service is compulsory, whereas in other countries serving in the army is _____________.

Enforcement

apprehend	corruption	function	obey	punish
code	enforced	lack	paper	

Having a reasonable law _____________ is not enough to ensure that a legal system will _____________ effectively. The laws may be fine on _____________, but that is not enough to ensure that the citizens will _____________ the law. Police must _____________ people who violate the law, and the courts must _____________ people who violate the law. _____________ is one reason that laws are not _____________. A _____________ of trained police officers, judges, and other court officials is another.

The first law codes

broke	draconian	Hammurabi's	penalties	tablets
codes	eye	injuring	preserved	

The first law _____________ were created thousands of years ago. Perhaps the most famous law code from the ancient world is _____________ law code, which is _____________ in numerous stone and clay _____________. In Hammurabi's code, the punishment for _____________ someone was to receive the same injury in return, or in other words, "an _____________ for an eye." Ancient law codes were often _____________, handing out severe _____________ to people who _____________ the law.

Idiom puzzle: Rules and laws idioms *Complete the following idioms. Use the shape symbols below the blanks to help you solve the idioms. Each symbol represents one letter.*

1. Sue a person: TAKE SOMEONE TO _ _ _ _ _
■ ♦ ◐ 1 ♣
2. Do something illegal: _ _ _ _ _ THE LAW
16 ♥ 22 ♠ Ω
3. The duty to show something is true: _ _ _ _ _ _ OF PROOF
★ 2 ♥ ▼ ▣ ▲
4. Follow the rules exactly: GO BY THE _ _ _ _
★ 20 ♦ Ω
5. Forcefully state the rules: LAY _ _ _ _ THE LAW
▼ ♦ ● 12
6. Exactly what the law says: THE _ _ _ _ _ _ OF THE LAW
∞ 17 ♣ ♣ ▣ ♥
7. Solid evidence of a wrongdoing: A _ _ _ _ _ _ _ GUN
♪ Σ 15 Ω Δ ▲ ◈
8. Prove somebody is innocent: _ _ _ _ _ SOMEONE'S NAME
■ ∞ ▣ ♠ 7
9. A cultural taboo: _ _ _ _ _ _ _ _ _ FRUIT
♦ 19 ★ Δ ▼ ▼ 10 ▲
10. Stay out of trouble: KEEP YOUR _ _ _ _ CLEAN
23 ♦ ♪ ▣
11. Illegal: _ _ _ _ _ _ _ THE LAW
11 ♠ Δ ▲ ♪ 13
12. Enforce the law severely: _ _ _ _ _ DOWN ON CRIME
■ ♥ ♠ ■ 21
13. Cause trouble: _ _ _ _ _ _ _ THE PEACE
▼ Δ ♪ 14 ◐ ♥ 18
14. A person who obeys the rules: A _ _ _-_ _ _ _ _ _ _ CITIZEN
3 ♠ ● ♠ ★ Δ ▼ Δ ▲ ◈
15. A general principle: A RULE OF _ _ _ _ _
♣ ◐ 9 ★
16. Exempt from legal punishment: _ _ _ _ _ THE LAW
6 ★ ♦ 4
17. According to the legal code: IN THE _ _ _ _ OF THE LAW
▣ ▣ 5
18. Disrespect toward the judge: _ _ _ _ _ _ _ _ OF COURT
■ ♦ ▲ ♣ 8 Σ ♣

PUZZLE 3·7

Code breaker *Use the number code in Puzzle 3•6 to solve the saying below.*

What disobedient people say:

_____ ___ _____ __ __ ______.

1 2 3 4 5   6 7 8   9 10 11 12 13   14 15   16 17   18 19 20 21 22 23

PUZZLE 3·8

Word paths: Laws, rules, and policies *Find and circle the secret words by following a connected path through the maze. Some words may overlap. Then solve the hidden message below.*

R	E	P	R	O	A	C	O	M	S	L
M		L		H		T		P		A
I	T	B	A	I	B	I	L	E	A	W
H		O		P		M		O		S
S	I	L	N	D	N	A	T	T	I	U
U		Y		A		S		H		I
N	E	R	O	T	R	E	P	E	A	L
B		W		R		V		I		L
I	Y	T	L	A	N	E	P	F	N	E
A		S		N		R		O		G
S	E	D	B	A	T	E	C	R	L	A

1. Forbid _ _ _ _ _ _ _ _
2. Legally get rid of something _ _ _ _ _ _ _
3. Compulsory _ _ _ _ _ _ _ _ _
4. Strict _ _ _ _ _ _
5. Allow _ _ _ _ _ _
6. Force someone to do something _ _ _ _ _ _
7. Cancel or rescind a law _ _ _ _ _ _
8. Punishment _ _ _ _ _ _ _
9. Against the law _ _ _ _ _ _ _
10. Make people obey the law _ _ _ _ _ _ _
11. A court case _ _ _ _ _ _ _
12. Fair and impartial _ _ _ _ _ _ _ _
13. Prohibit _ _ _

Hidden message: An idiom about punishment *Use the remaining letters to uncover an idiom related to feelings and emotions.*

A very lenient punishment:

_   _ _ _ _   _ _   _ _ _   _ _ _ _ _

PUZZLE
3·9

Crossword: Rules and laws

Across

1. Allow.
4. Legal.
5. Free from obligation or liability that is imposed on others.
7. Pass (a law).
8. Punishment.
10. Enforce the law severely: ______ down on crime.
12. Must be done.
15. Commit a crime: ______ the law.
19. Something people follow.

Down

1. The responsibility to show something is true: Burden of ______.
2. Cancel a law.
3. Unbiased and fair.
4. Lenient.
6. A person who is not legally an adult.
9. Not allowed.
11. A collection of laws.
12. Obey a rule or law.
13. The time when you are legally an adult: The age of ______.

Across

21. Exactly what the law says: _______ of the law.
22. Do what the law says.
24. A court case.
25. Prohibit.
26. Legal responsibility for a violation of the law.

Down

14. Take someone to court.
16. Not against the rules.
17. Limit.
18. Against the law.
20. Forbid.
23. A rule created by governments.

Word scramble: Rules and laws *Use the clues to unscramble the letters and form words used to discuss rules and laws.*

1. Pass a law:	E C N A T	_ _ _ _ _	22, 13
2. Not strict or harsh:	N L E E I T N	_ _ _ _ _ _ _	4, 10
3. Forbid:	H P I B R O I T	_ _ _ _ _ _ _ _	24, 27
4. Permit:	W O L L A	_ _ _ _ _	17, 23
5. Force:	P E L M O C	_ _ _ _ _ _	1, 7
6. Strict or harsh:	V R E E S E	_ _ _ _ _ _	3, 11
7. A collection of laws:	D C O E	_ _ _ _	2, 29
8. Officially put an end to something:	B O A L I H S	_ _ _ _ _ _ _	15, 21
9. Do what the law says:	B E Y O	_ _ _ _	18, 6
10. Legal:	F U L L A W	_ _ _ _ _ _	28, 8
11. Solid evidence of wrongdoing (two words):	K O S M G N I N U G	_ _ _ _ _ _ _ _ _ _	26, 14
12. A court case:	T U I S A W L	_ _ _ _ _ _ _	12, 19
13. Fair and unbiased:	P A R I M T I A L	_ _ _ _ _ _ _ _ _	25, 5
14. Prohibit:	N A B	_ _ _	16
15. Put a limit on something:	S T R I R E C T	_ _ _ _ _ _ _ _	9, 20

Code breaker *Use the number code in Puzzle 3•10 to solve the idioms related to following the law.*

Idiom 1

Hide your wrongdoing:

__ __ __ __ __   __ __ __ __   __ __ __ __ __ __
1 2 3 4 5   6 7 8 9   10 11 12 13 14 15

Idiom 2

Reveal someone else's wrongdoing:

__ __ __ __   __ __ __   __ __ __ __ __ __ __
16 17 18 19   20 21 22   23 24 25 26 27 28 29

Crime and punishment ·4·

VOCABULARY

armed robbery
arson
assault
blackmail
bribery
burglary
computer hacking
dealing narcotics
driving intoxicated
identity theft
illegal downloading
jaywalking
kidnapping
littering
murder/homicide
perjury
pickpocketing
possession of narcotics
public intoxication
shoplifting
smuggling
speeding
tax evasion
vandalism

PUZZLE **4·1**

Definition match-up: Crime and punishment *Match the following definitions with words from the vocabulary list. More than one word may fit some of the definitions.*

1. Stealing from a store: ________________
2. Breaking into a home to steal: ________________
3. Driving after drinking alcohol: ________________
4. Selling illegal drugs: ________________
5. Carrying a small amount of drugs on you: ________________
6. Walking across a street illegally: ________________
7. Threatening to reveal a secret unless somebody pays you: ________________
8. Destroying public property: ________________
9. Throwing garbage on the ground: ________________
10. Using a weapon to steal: ________________
11. Driving too fast: ________________
12. Lying under oath: ________________
13. Punching or kicking someone: ________________
14. Lying to the government about how much money you earned: ________________

15. Illegally giving money to someone so that he or she will do you a favor: ______________________

16. Lighting a building on fire: ______________________

PUZZLE

4·2

Word sort: Types of crime *A* felony *is a very serious crime. The punishment for a felony is often prison in excess of one year. A* misdemeanor *is a less serious crime. The punishment for misdemeanors is usually a fine, community service, or a jail sentence of less than one year.*

In your opinion, which of the crimes in the vocabulary list should be considered felonies and which of them should be misdemeanors? Choose 12 crimes and rewrite them in the table.

FELONIES	MISDEMEANORS
______________________	______________________
______________________	______________________
______________________	______________________

PUZZLE

4·3

Labeling: Crime and punishment *Attach the following labels to the lists of words below.*

Criminals in general	Evidence	Sentences
Criminals who destroy property	Investigation procedures	Verdicts
Criminals who steal	People at a trial	Where criminals are kept

1. culprit, offender, outlaw, perpetrator ______________________
2. burglar, robber, shoplifter, thief ______________________
3. guilty, innocent ______________________
4. arsonist, hacker, vandal ______________________
5. cell, jail, prison ______________________
6. interrogate, interview, gather evidence ______________________
7. (the) accused, attorney, (the) judge, (the) jury, prosecutor, witness ______________________
8. bloodstain, DNA, fingerprint, (video) footage, footprint, hair, testimony ______________________
9. time (in prison), fine, (community) service ______________________

PUZZLE 4·4

Word search: Crime and punishment *Find the following words (from Puzzle 4·3) in the grid.*

```
S H O P L I F T E R I N T E R V I E W A L L
T E S T I M O N Y T A T T O R N E Y H A T I
S E N T E N C E S I N E C E A R S O N I S T
B L O O D S T A I N P E R P E T R A T O R S
S J U T H I E F A V F I N G E R P R I N T R
Y U T F O R T H E E T R C U L P R I T I U M
A D L P H O F E V S I L I S T C H A R G E H
R G A J U R Y A T T I N T E R R O G A T E T
R E W G O O D T R I A L H M E N D N O N N O
E I N N O C E N T G P T B A F I N E V I H Y
S W I T N E S S I A R N G U I A T E R I T L
T E V A N D A L L T I L M E R R C P W L C H
O Y R O U R F L R E S T I M E G T C I I E T
D N D V S A E R E A O N D B I O L U U W I L
N L T E I C J A I L N L B L O Y G A O S U W
A H O H A C K E R Y O O F F E N D E R U E A
F O O T A G E R E P R O S E C U T O R Q Q D
```

accused
arrest
arsonist
attorney
bloodstain
burglar
cell
charge
convict
culprit
DNA
fine
fingerprint
footage
footprint
guilty
hacker
hair
innocent
interrogate
interview
investigate
jail
judge
jury
offender
outlaw
perpetrator
prison
prosecutor
robber
sentence
service
shoplifter
testimony
thief
time
trial
vandal
witness

Hidden messages *Once you have found all of the words in Puzzle 4•4, the remaining letters form two hidden messages. Uncover the messages and fill in the blanks below.*

Quotation

___ ____ __ _________ ___ ___

_______ __ ____ __ ____ ____ ___ __

_______.

—Edmund Burke

Proverb

____ __ ___ ____ _______ ___

___ _ ____ ____ ___ ___ ___ ___.

—Assyrian Proverb

Word paths: Criminals *Find and circle the secret words by following a connected path through the maze. Some words may overlap.*

B	A	N	D	I	T	H	I	E	F	V
H	■	C	■	R	■	A	■	E	■	A
G	B	U	L	P	I	C	K	P	O	N
T	■	R	■	R	■	K	■	O	■	D
C	A	G	L	A	U	E	G	C	L	A
S	■	H	■	T	■	R	■	K	■	R
H	O	P	E	R	O	B	D	E	T	A
H	■	L	■	E	■	B	■	A	■	R
N	D	I	F	T	E	E	R	D	P	I

1. A person who steals things. _ _ _ _ _
2. A person who breaks into homes. _ _ _ _ _ _ _
3. A person who destroys property. _ _ _ _ _ _
4. A person who steals from stores. _ _ _ _ _ _ _ _ _ _
5. A person who steals from banks. _ _ _ _ _ _
6. A person who breaks into computers. _ _ _ _ _ _
7. A person who steals your wallet on the subway. _ _ _ _ _ _ _ _ _ _
8. A person who attacks people in ships. _ _ _ _ _ _
9. Another word for perpetrator. _ _ _ _ _ _ _
10. A person who robs you when you are traveling in the mountains or forest. _ _ _ _ _ _

Hidden message: Crime idiom *Use the remaining letters to uncover a crime idiom.*

Did you read the article about the paint thief in the morning paper?

_ _   _ _ _   _ _ _ _ _ _   _ _ _-_ _ _ _ _ _ _ _.

PUZZLE 4·7

Word sort: Police investigations and criminal trials *The following words and phrases are often associated with investigating crimes and putting criminals on trial. Sort these words and phrases into the three categories shown.*

the accused	fingerprints	investigate	sentence
arrest	footprints	the judge	surveillance video
bloodstains	fugitive	the jury	suspect
charge	gunshot residue	police officer	testimony
detective	interrogate	prosecutor	victim
DNA	interview	put on trial	witness

EVIDENCE	PROCEDURES	PEOPLE INVOLVED
______	______	______
______	______	______
______	______	______
______	______	______
______	______	______

PUZZLE 4·8

Definition match-up: People involved in criminal proceedings *Match the following definitions with the vocabulary words. Words may be used more than once, and definitions may have several words that match.*

the accused	fugitive	perpetrator	victim
criminal	judge	police officer	witness
culprit	jury	prosecutor	
detective	outlaw	suspect	

1. somebody who commits a crime: ______
2. a person who has seen a crime: ______
3. someone who investigates crimes: ______
4. a group of people that hears testimony at a trial: ______
5. a person who suffered because of a crime: ______
6. someone who is running away from the law: ______
7. a person who hands down sentences: ______
8. someone who gives testimony at a trial: ______
9. a person who has been put on trial: ______
10. a person who presents evidence: ______

PUZZLE 4·9

Fill in the blanks: Collocating prepositions *Fill in the blank with a collocating preposition.*

1. accuse somebody ______________ a crime
2. acquit somebody ______________ a crime
3. arrest somebody ______________ a crime
4. charge somebody ______________ a crime
5. convict somebody ______________ a crime
6. punish somebody ______________ a crime
7. put somebody ______________ jail
8. put somebody ______________ trial
9. sentence someone ______________ life in prison
10. serve time ______________ a crime
11. suspect somebody ______________ a crime

PUZZLE 4·10

Fill in the blanks: Criminal investigations *Complete the following paragraphs by filling in the blanks using the words provided.*

Crimes

against	investigation	shoplifting	victim
committed	perpetrator	vandalism	

Crimes are things people do that are ______________ the law. Crimes include things such as ______________, which is the destruction of public property, and ______________, which is stealing from a store. A ______________ is a person who has suffered from a crime. When a crime is ______________, the police open an ______________ in order to catch the ______________.

Investigations

alibi	evidence	scene	witnesses
breaks	interrogate	suspects	

When somebody ______________ the law, the police go to the crime ______________ and gather ______________. During their investigations, the police talk to ______________ and ask what they saw. The police use the evidence and witness testimony to make a list of possible _____________, or people they think may have committed the crime. The police then _____________ the suspects to see if they have an _____________.

Arrests

arrest	charge	handcuffs
cell	fugitives	resist

When the police think they have enough evidence to _____________ a suspect with a crime, they locate the suspect and make an _____________. This can be a dangerous time because some suspects _____________ the arrest violently or flee from the police. If suspects flee, they become _____________. Often, the police use _____________ to control the suspects until they get them to the police station. The suspects are held in a jail _____________ until trial.

Trials

accused	jury	testimony
innocent	sentence	trial

Suspects who have been charged with crimes are put on _____________. The suspect is now called the _____________. During the trial, a _____________ listens to evidence gathered by the police and the _____________ of witnesses. The jury then decides if the defendant is _____________ or guilty. If the jury finds the defendant guilty, the judge hands down a _____________.

Punishment

armed	convicted	fine	prison
community	felonies	misdemeanors	serve

When people are _____________ of a crime, they receive a sentence as punishment. The punishment that is handed down will depend on the seriousness of the crime. People convicted of _____________ such as murder or _____________ robbery usually _____________ long periods of time in _____________. People convicted of _____________ such as shoplifting usually are not sentenced to time in jail, but instead are required to pay a _____________ or do _____________ service.

Word scramble: Guilty verdict *Find the words described below within the phrase "guilty verdict." You can use the letters in any order, but you can only use each letter once.*

GUILTY VERDICT

HINT: USE THE CODE BREAKER TO THE RIGHT TO HELP YOU SOLVE THE WORDS. ANY TIME NUMBERS IN THE CODE ARE REPEATED, LETTERS IN THE CORRESPONDING WORDS ARE REPEATED AS WELL.

CLUES	ANSWERS	CODE BREAKER
1. An animal with stripes.	_ _ _ _ _	1 x 2 x 23
2. The opposite of good.	_ _ _ _	x 3 x 4
3. Another word for heal.	_ _ _ _	5 6 23 x
4. A way to lose weight.	_ _ _ _	7 x x 8
5. Garbage on the ground.	_ _ _ _ _ _	9 x 10 10 x x
6. The opposite of take.	_ _ _ _	11 12 x x
7. A place where many people live.	_ _ _ _	5 x 8 13
8. Another word for hint.	_ _ _ _	14 9 x x
9. A staple crop in Asia.	_ _ _ _	16 x 15 x
10. Another word for soil.	_ _ _ _	17 x x 18
11. An animal with a shell.	_ _ _ _ _ _	8 19 x x x x
12. The opposite of false.	_ _ _ _	18 16 x x
13. Something sticky.	_ _ _ _	11 4 x x
14. A fight between two people.	_ _ _ _	7 20 26 x
15. Fix an essay.	_ _ _ _	21 x x 1
16. Forks, spoons, and knives.	_ _ _ _ _ _ _	15 6 1 x x 22 13
17. What you do with a car.	_ _ _ _ _	x x x 3 21
18. The opposite of polite.	_ _ _ _	x 19 x 26
19. The opposite of boy.	_ _ _ _	25 x 22 x
20. Someone who shows you the way.	_ _ _ _ _	2 6 x 17 x
21. The opposite of messy.	_ _ _ _	10 x x 24
22. Something you roll in a game.	_ _ _ _	x 12 14 x
23. Another word for carpet.	_ _ _	x 20 25
24. The opposite of wet.	_ _ _	x 23 24

Crossword: Crime and punishment

Across

4. A person who destroys public property.
5. The people who decide whether a person is guilty or innocent.
7. A person who sells drugs.
10. A person who presides over a court.
12. A person who catches criminals.
14. A place where trials are held.
15. "Get _______ with a crime": Not get punished for committing a crime.

Down

1. A mark you leave when you touch something.
2. Things that prove somebody committed a crime.
3. The crime of using a weapon to steal from someone: _______ robbery.
6. A criminal who breaks into a building to steal.
8. The crime of lighting a building on fire.
9. A serious crime.

Across

17. The process of determining if a person is innocent or guilty.
21. Theft, robbery, or murder.
22. Interview a suspect.
24. A story that proves your innocence.
26. A high-ranking police officer who solves serious crimes.
27. Another word for criminal.
31. A person who has committed a crime.
32. A person who the police think may have done a crime.

Down

11. The punishment a judge hands down.
13. A rule made by the government.
16. Captured by the police.
18. A spot of blood.
19. Evidence taken from blood or saliva.
20. A person who has suffered from a crime.
23. The crime of stealing.
24. The crime of attacking someone.
25. "______ the law": Commit a crime
28. A place where criminals are kept.
29. Say somebody committed a crime.
30. Money paid as punishment for breaking the law.

Journalism and mass media

VOCABULARY

advertisement	editorial	print media
anchor	exaggerate	propaganda
article	exposé	scandal
biased/one-sided	front page	sensationalist
blog	headlines	sources
blogosphere	investigative	spin
broadcast media	journalist	tabloid
censorship	objective	verify
column	the press	watchdog
correspondent	press conference	
coverage	press release	

PUZZLE **5·1**

Definition match-up: Journalism and mass media *Match the following definitions with words from the vocabulary list. More than one word may fit some of the definitions.*

1. Any news story: ____________________
2. A news article that appears regularly: ____________________
3. A news article that presents an opinion: ____________________
4. An article, book, or show that reveals a scandal or crime to the public: ____________________
5. The amount and quality of reporting that an issue gets: ____________________
6. TV and radio: ____________________
7. Newspapers, magazines, and books: ____________________
8. A person who writes news articles: ____________________
9. The title of a news article (though also used to refer to the important articles themselves): ____________________

10. The area of a newspaper reserved for the most important news: ______________________

11. Favoring one particular point of view: ______________________

12. The opposite of biased: ______________________

13. News put out by the government to make the government look good: ______________________

14. A form of propaganda/bias where facts are manipulated to give a positive (or negative) interpretation of a story: ______________________

15. Shocking or outrageous reporting meant to increase readership or viewership: ______________________

16. A type of newspaper that is often sensationalist: ______________________

17. Confirm that something is accurate and true: ______________________

18. The prohibition of printing or airing something: ______________________

19. Places or people where information is obtained: ______________________

20. An official statement issued to newspapers: ______________________

PUZZLE 5·2

Labeling: Media *Attach the following media-related labels to the lists of words that follow.*

Broadcast media	Government-controlled media	Print media
Free press	Online media	Sensationalist media

1. scandals, shocking events ______________________
2. e-zine, blog ______________________
3. independent, unbiased ______________________
4. radio, television ______________________
5. censorship, propaganda ______________________
6. newspaper, magazine ______________________

Fill in the blanks: Journalism and mass media *Complete the following paragraphs by filling in the blanks using the words provided.*

Types of media

blog	newspapers	professional
broadcast	online	quality
media	print	radio

The means of mass communication we use are called the ____________. The oldest form of media is ____________ media, which includes books, ____________, and magazines. Another type of media is called ____________ media, which includes TV, film, and ____________. In the last few decades a new form of media, ____________ media, has revolutionized communication. In the past, print and broadcast media were dominated by ____________ journalists working for large networks, but now just about anyone can write a ____________ and upload it to the Internet. Of course, some critics worry that ____________ is being replaced by quantity.

Principles of journalism

biased	other	sources
minds	sensationalist	verify
objective	sides	

Good journalism is ____________, which means journalists should not be influenced by their personal feelings or favor one side of an issue over the other. In ____________ words, good journalism should not be ____________ or one-sided. Journalists should try to present both ____________ of an issue so that members of the public can make up their own ____________. Good journalism is also truthful. Journalists should ____________ their facts and collect information from multiple ____________. Finally, good journalism should not be ____________, which means journalists shouldn't twist facts or print shocking stories just to increase their readership.

The media as a watchdog

corruption	independent	order
eye	inefficiency	polluting
function	investigative	watchdog

In democratic countries, one important ____________ of the media is to act as a ____________, protecting the public interests. For example, the media can expose government ____________ by revealing politicians who take bribes. The media can also expose government ____________ by reporting on wasteful expenditures of taxpayers' money. The media also keeps a watchful ____________ on businesses and exposes corporate wrongdoing such as ______________ the environment. This kind of journalism is sometimes called ______________ journalism. In ______________ to carry out this important function, the media needs to be ______________ and not under the control of business and government.

Censorship

aired	free	slander
censorship	incite	speech
criticism	profanity	

Prohibiting something from being published or ______________ by the mass media because it is objectionable is called ______________. In some countries, any ______________ of the government gets censored because the government is worried about holding onto power. In other countries, things that the government finds morally objectionable such as ______________ or nudity may be censored. Democratic countries, which tend to value the ______________ press and freedom of ______________, usually limit censorship. But even in democratic countries, you cannot say whatever you want. You cannot ______________ somebody and ruin his or her reputation, nor can you ______________ others to violence.

PUZZLE 5·4

Crossword: Journalism and mass media

Across

1. An online journal.
3. The amount and quality of reporting that an issue gets.
4. An official statement issued to newspapers: A press ______.
5. Negative comments about someone.
7. A type of print media that comes daily.
8. Where some information comes from.
10. Another way to say unbiased.

Down

1. TV and radio: ______ media.
2. The prohibition of printing or airing something.
3. A series of regularly occurring articles (usually by one person).
6. Biased information used to promote a particular political point of view.
9. A person who reads the news on TV.
10. Not controlled by government.
11. Favoring one particular point of view.

Across (cont.)

12. A type of broadcast media that you listen to.
13. A person who supplies news stories to the media.
15. The news media.
18. A news article that presents someone's opinion.
23. A person who writes news articles.
24. A news story in a magazine or newspaper.
25. Something that ruins someone's reputation without proof.

Down (cont.)

14. Newspapers and magazines: ______ media.
16. Something that causes public outrage.
17. The title of a newspaper article.
19. Not influenced by personal feelings.
20. A type of newspaper associated with sensationalist stories.
21. A place where important stories are printed: The ______ page.
22. Make sure that something is true.

PUZZLE 5·5

Word search: Media *Find the following words in the grid.*

M	M	H	A	X	I	N	T	E	R	V	I	E	W	J	O	U	R	N	A	L	I	S	T
G	U	W	M	H	S	K	W	T	P	R	O	P	A	G	A	N	D	A	B	G	J	D	C
V	Q	E	F	A	R	P	S	E	N	S	A	T	I	O	N	A	L	I	S	T	E	U	E
Z	T	V	I	O	I	A	R	V	T	B	Q	T	I	N	D	E	P	E	N	D	E	N	T
B	M	B	W	E	C	N	R	E	P	O	R	T	E	R	O	F	F	E	N	S	I	V	E
U	G	T	S	D	I	G	S	K	S	P	R	E	S	S	R	E	L	E	A	S	E	T	D
D	E	F	A	D	V	E	R	T	I	S	E	M	E	N	T	C	O	L	U	M	N	A	K
N	Y	O	G	E	E	S	Z	H	R	H	C	B	M	Z	M	A	S	S	M	E	D	I	A
T	R	B	F	Z	U	P	Z	E	U	E	V	O	M	A	G	P	U	B	L	I	S	H	K
B	Q	J	K	F	S	R	S	P	X	U	A	Q	N	O	C	O	V	E	R	A	G	E	A
R	U	E	M	W	S	I	C	R	Z	R	Y	M	L	F	M	A	G	A	Z	I	N	E	A
A	N	C	H	O	R	N	A	E	I	J	A	B	B	K	E	I	N	F	O	R	M	E	D
H	F	T	W	Z	I	T	N	S	M	P	E	D	I	T	O	R	I	A	L	S	I	E	Y
L	J	I	D	P	F	M	D	S	E	X	P	O	S	E	N	J	E	W	J	U	F	M	N
F	Z	V	S	X	W	E	A	H	V	E	R	I	F	Y	E	C	E	N	S	O	R	C	I
L	U	E	H	E	A	D	L	I	N	E	S	R	B	L	W	W	A	T	C	H	D	O	G
X	R	G	M	A	N	I	P	U	L	A	T	E	O	E	S	O	U	R	C	E	S	H	V
A	L	T	E	R	N	A	T	I	V	E	L	F	J	G	M	H	T	A	B	L	O	I	D

advertisement
air
alternative
anchor
bias
blog
broadcast
censor
column

coverage
editorial
exposé
headlines
independent
informed
interview
journalist
magazine
mainstream
manipulate
mass media
network
news
objective
offensive
press conference
press release
print media
propaganda
publish
reporter
scandal
sensationalist
sources
spin
tabloid
the press
verify
watchdog

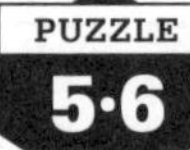

Word paths: Journalism and the mass media *Find and circle the secret words by following a connected path through the maze. Some words may overlap.*

H	E	A	B	V	E	R	I	F	Y	M
E		D		A		E		D		A
N	I	L	O	G	N	N	I	Z	A	G
O		B		E		W		S		T
B	J	E	N	S	O	R	O	N	T	P
R		C		A		F		V		A
V	I	T	R	O	H	C	N	A	E	G
E		E		L		L		S		F
T	O	R	I	A	B	L	O	I	D	S
I		A		T		S		T		J
D	E	T	E	I	L	A	N	R	U	O

1. A person who writes news articles. _ _ _ _ _ _ _ _ _ _ _ _ _
2. An article that expresses an opinion. _ _ _ _ _ _ _ _ _ _ _ _
3. The title of an article. _ _ _ _ _ _ _ _ _ _ _

4. Not influenced by personal feelings. _ _ _ _ _ _ _ _ _ _ _
5. Confirm that something is true. _ _ _ _ _ _ _
6. A form of print media that comes monthly. _ _ _ _ _ _ _ _ _
7. An online journal. _ _ _ _
8. Prohibit something from being printed. _ _ _ _ _ _ _
9. A place for important stories (two words). _ _ _ _ _ _ _ _ _ _
10. Someone who hosts a news broadcast. _ _ _ _ _ _ _
11. Newspapers known for sensationalist news. _ _ _ _ _ _ _ _ _

Hidden message: A proverb about the media *Use the remaining letters to uncover a phrase related to the media.*

If something tragic happened, you would have heard about it already.

_ _ _   _ _ _ _   _ _ _ _ _ _ _ _   _ _ _ _

Government and elections ·6·

VOCABULARY

ballot	endorsement	political party
campaign contribution	exit poll	poll
candidate	incumbent	polling booth
coalition	landslide	smear campaign
constituent	majority	speech
dark horse	nonpartisan	vote
debate	plank	voter
election	platform	
election campaign	political opponent	

PUZZLE 6·1

Definition match-up: Government and elections *Match the following definitions with words from the vocabulary list. More than one word may fit some of the definitions.*

1. A person who runs for government: ____________________
2. Someone a candidate has to beat in an election: ____________________
3. A group of politicians and supporters with similar aims and beliefs: ____________________
4. Money given to a political party by a supporter: ____________________
5. The group of activities such as speeches and ads that candidates use to get elected: ____________________
6. A campaign that attacks the character of a political opponent: ____________________
7. All of the goals or aims of a candidate or party: ____________________
8. One goal or aim of a candidate: ____________________
9. An announcement of support for a candidate: ____________________
10. A piece of paper on which voters mark their choice: ____________________
11. A talk that candidates give to a crowd: ____________________

12. The current holder of a government office: ______________

13. An event where candidates argue against each other to gain voter support: ______________

14. A survey to find out how people will vote: ______________

15. A place where people cast their vote: ______________

16. A survey to find out who people voted for after they come out of the polling booth: ______________

17. More than 50 percent of the vote: ______________

18. An overwhelming victory in an election: ______________

19. A government formed by the combination of more than one political party: ______________

20. An unknown candidate who does surprisingly well: ______________

PUZZLE **6·2**

Collocation match-up: Election collocations *Match the election words in the vocabulary list with their collocations below.*

cast	exit	opposition	smear
coalition	free	party	swing
dark	landslide	run	voter

1. ____________ party
2. ____________ turnout
3. ____________ government
4. ____________ victory
5. ____________ your vote
6. ____________ horse
7. ____________ for office
8. ____________ campaign
9. ____________ platform
10. ____________ elections
11. ____________ polls
12. ____________ voter

PUZZLE 6·3

Fill in the blanks: Elections *Complete the following paragraphs by filling in the blanks using the words provided.*

Candidates

candidates	elections	independents	party
democratic	incumbent	opponent	reelected

In ____________ countries, citizens vote for their government in ____________. The people who run for government are called ____________. Most candidates belong to a political ____________. Candidates who do not belong to a party are called ____________. A person whom a candidate is trying to beat in an election is that candidate's political ____________, or rival. The person who currently holds the government office is called the ____________. If an incumbent wants to keep his or her office for another term, the incumbent has to get ____________.

Political parties

issue	platform	toe
leader	political	winning

A ____________ party is an organization of people with similar beliefs about how government should be run. Political parties try to get power by ____________ elections. The collection of aims of a political party is the party ____________. The most powerful member of a party is known as the party ____________. Members of a political party are often expected to ____________ the party line, which means they are supposed to vote with the party no matter how they feel about a particular ____________.

Election campaigns

ads	character	opponents	speeches
campaign	debates	smear	support

An election ____________ is a series of activities that candidates take part in before an election to gain voter ____________. An election campaign can involve placing ____________ on TV, giving ____________ in public or participating in ____________ with political ____________. Sometimes, candidates say nasty things about an opponent or place ads that attack the ____________ of an opponent. This kind of campaign is known as a ____________ campaign.

Election day

booths	counted	recount
cast	polls	turnout

On election day, people head to polling ____________ to ____________ their ballots. The ballots are then collected and ____________ to determine who the winner is. Usually, exit ____________ indicate who will win, even before the votes are counted. If many people show up to vote, we say there is high voter ____________. Sometimes, if the vote is very close, there can be a ____________ to make sure the tally is accurate.

PUZZLE 6·4

Crossword: Government and elections

Across

1. The collection of aims and beliefs of a political party.
6. A voter that changes his or her mind: a ______ voter.
7. An event where candidates present their views and argue with opponents.
9. Cast your ballot.
10. Choose whom you want to win: ______ your vote.
11. A survey to see whom people are going to vote for.
14. An announcement of support for a candidate (often by a famous or powerful person).
16. The number of voters who show up to vote: Voter ______.
17. Do what your party says: ______ the line.
19. Try to get elected: ______ for office.
21. A political party that supports the environment.
22. A person who is running for government.

Down

1. An organization that has shared beliefs about government and tries to get elected.
2. Over 50 percent of the vote.
3. Money given to a candidate: A campaign ______.
4. Win by a large margin: A ______ victory.
5. A candidate that doesn't belong to a party.
8. A piece of paper where voters can mark their choice.
10. A government made of more than one political party.
12. A time when people vote for their government.
13. A campaign that attacks an opponent's character: ______ campaign.
15. A series of actions such as placing ads, giving speeches, and participating in debates in order to get elected.
18. Somebody a candidate is trying to beat in an election.
20. A talk that candidates give in public.

PUZZLE **6·5**

Word search: Elections *Find the following words in the grid.*

```
C A N D I D A T E E I N D E P E N D E N T E U N
E Z D R X Z P Y P W J D F E Y F I N I N U G E O
S T P C G S U A F B H S R N X D T P L I D I N Y
D E N D O R S E M E N T L B X N S J G W Z W R M
E V H N V A C C M W F F W D E M O C R A C Y O L
B Y X O E D O B O H V B O B V W H U D L H G E V
A U M O R U N Z I N V L M A E C M N A Y B I E F
T B O D N H T S M T S U S L T Z A C E P L T S N
E E S T M G R B X U C T G L O S I P B V Y Y G X
J L R Z E Q I S V N G I I O I T Y L N T N I T C
L H T I N J B V I P O L I T I C I A N D A V R A
M B W E T Q U G C A S T R L U T M N L P R R W G
A C O A L I T I O N U A O I D E P K M H T Y Z S
Y M A J O R I T Y U P P D R V X N A N Y Y B T L
O P L A T F O R M N C V O J J A C T E R F Z F U
R S M E A R N V O S O R O L Z E L E C T I O N N
G L O A K W P N P A R T Y T L A N D S L I D E U
D A R K H O R S E O C P Y U E O P P O N E N T Y
```

ballot
campaign
candidate
cast
coalition
constituent
contribution
dark horse
debate
democracy
election
endorsement
government
incumbent
independent
landslide
majority
mayor
nonpartisan
opponent
party
plank
platform
political
politician
poll
rival
smear
spin
veto
vote

Idiom puzzle: Election idioms and expressions *Complete the election-related idioms below. Use the symbols below the blanks to help you solve the idioms.*

Clue	Idiom	Symbols
1. Try to get elected:	RUN FOR _ _ _ _ _ _	14 ♥ ♥ 31 ▼ 10
2. Travel around the country to gain votes:	HIT THE _ _ _ _ _ _ _ _ TRAIL	▼ ♦ Σ ◐ 11 36 Δ Ω
3. Vote in an election:	CAST YOUR _ _ _ _ _ _	21 ♣ 13 ● ★
4. An election day rival:	A POLITICAL _ _ _ _ _ _ _ _	● ◐ ◐ 43 6 ■ Ω 38
5. Speak on and on about an issue:	GET ON YOUR _ _ _ _ _ _ _	34 ● ♦ 9 24
6. A close race:	A _ _ _ _ HEAT	■ 40 16
7. The number of people who voted:	VOTER _ _ _ _ _ _ _	★ ♠ 25 44 ● ♠ ★
8. What some candidates do:	_ _ _ _ _ _ _ THE WORLD	◐ 33 ● Σ ▣ 7 ■
9. An unknown candidate:	A _ _ _ _ HORSE	26 ♦ ▲ 12
10. A win by a wide margin:	A _ _ _ _ _ _ _ _ _ VICTORY	♣ 35 Ω 42 27 ♣ ▣ 37 17
11. An attack on an opponent's character:	A _ _ _ _ _ CAMPAIGN	◈ Σ 32 1 ▲
12. Try to hide something embarrassing:	_ _ _ _ _ UP A SCANDAL	20 ♠ ◈ 39
13. What you do in partisan politics:	_ _ _ THE PARTY LINE	★ ● 28
14. Cheat in an election:	_ _ _ _ _ THE BALLOT BOX	30 ★ 15 ♥ ♥
15. Give up in an election:	THROW IN THE _ _ _ _ _	★ 5 23 ■ ♣
16. Offensive to women or minorities:	POLITICALLY _ _ _ _ _ _ _ _ _	▣ 41 2 ● ▲ ▲ ■ ▼ 19
17. A voter that may change his or her mind:	A _ _ _ _ _ VOTER	8 4 Ω Δ
18. What a political party says it will do:	THE PARTY _ _ _ _ _ _ _ _	◐ ♣ 29 3 ♥ ● 18 Σ
19. What some candidates do when they win:	_ _ _ _ _ _ ON PROMISES	▲ ■ 22 ■ Δ 45

Code breaker: Two proverbs *Use the number code in Puzzle 6•6 to discover the two proverbs.*

Proverb 1

What people do is more important than what they say:

_ _ _ _ _ _ _   _ _ _ _ _   _ _ _ _ _ _   _ _ _ _   _ _ _ _ _.

1 2 3 4 5 6 7   8 9 10 11 12   13 14 15 16 17 18   19 20 21 22   23 24 25 26 27

Proverb 2

Sounds simple to do but isn't in practice:

_ _ _ _ _ _   _ _ _ _   _ _ _ _   _ _ _ _.

28 29 30 31 32 33   34 35 36 37   38 39 40 41   42 43 44 45

Disease and medicine

·7·

VOCABULARY

antibiotics
bacteria
benign
checkup
chronic
contagious
cure
diagnosis
epidemic
fungus
germs
lump
immune system
immunization
infection
painkiller
parasite
pathogens
patient
prescription
relieve
specialist
surgery
symptom
treatment
tumor
vaccines
virus

PUZZLE 7·1

Definition match-up: Disease and medicine *Match the following definitions with words from the vocabulary list.*

1. Microorganisms that cause disease such as bacteria, viruses, and parasites: ______________________
2. The parts of your body that fight infection: ______________________
3. A doctor who treats only one type of illness: ______________________
4. Medicines that kill unwanted bacteria or fungi: ______________________
5. Substances that provide immunity to diseases: ______________________
6. Can spread from person to person: ______________________
7. A sign of an illness: ______________________
8. The identification of an illness by a doctor: ______________________
9. A condition whereby germs have entered your body: ______________________
10. A disease that has spread widely: ______________________
11. Not damaging to health: ______________________
12. A person who seeks medical attention: ______________________
13. The process of getting vaccinated: ______________________
14. Heal an illness: ______________________

15. Make a symptom bearable: ___________________________

16. An illness that comes back again and again: ___________________________

17. An abnormal growth of a tissue: ___________________________

18. A routine visit to the doctor to make sure you are healthy: ___________________________

PUZZLE **7·2**

Labeling: Disease and medicine *Attach the following disease- and medicine-related labels to the lists of words that follow.*

Cold symptoms	Injuries	Remedies
Contagious diseases	Medical professionals	Skin ailments
Diagnosis aids	Preventive measures	Types of infection

1. bacterial, fungal, viral ___________________________
2. cough, runny nose, sore throat ___________________________
3. sunburn, insect bite, rash ___________________________
4. blood samples, patient interviews, x-rays ___________________________
5. antibiotics, painkillers, surgery ___________________________
6. broken bone, sprained ankle, torn ligament ___________________________
7. cholera, influenza, strep throat ___________________________
8. pediatrician, pharmacist, surgeon ___________________________
9. eating a balanced diet, frequent hand washing, immunizations ___________________________

PUZZLE **7·3**

Fill in the blanks: Disease and medicine *Complete the following paragraphs by filling in the blanks using the words provided.*

A visit to the doctor

blood	health	specialist
diagnosis	opinion	symptoms
general	prescription	treatment

If you are ill or worried about your _______________ and it is not an emergency, you usually visit a family doctor, or a _______________ practitioner. Your doctor will examine and interview you to find out what _______________ you have. Your doctor may also order some tests such as a ______________ sample or an x-ray. Your doctor will then use the results of the interview and the tests to make a ______________. Once a diagnosis is made, the doctor can begin ______________. If the doctor feels that your condition is not serious, he or she may just write you a ______________ for medicine and tell you to get some rest. However, if the doctor cannot diagnose what is wrong or the doctor feels your condition is serious, he or she may refer you to a ______________. At any rate, if the diagnosis is serious, it is always good to get a second ______________.

The immune system

eradicate	medicine	vaccinations
immune	parasites	viruses
infections	tuberculosis	

The purpose of your immune system is to fight off ______________ from pathogens such as bacteria, ______________, fungi, and ______________. Though your immune system can often take care of an infection on its own, we sometimes take ______________ to help our immune system fight an illness and shorten its duration. Indeed, there are some illnesses, such as ______________, that your immune system may not be able to overcome without medicine. The immune system must be able to recognize a variety of pathogens to function properly. We can aid this process through ______________. A vaccine is a substance that contains a weakened form of a disease. Vaccines stimulate the immune system to recognize and destroy that substance and then "remember" it so that you will be ______________ to that disease in the future. Health experts around the world hope that vaccination programs can ______________ some of the worst forms of contagious disease.

Cure and relief

antibiotics	cure	purposes	sore
bearable	fungal	relieve	

Different medicines serve different ______________. Some medicines are meant to help ______________ diseases. For example, ______________ can kill bacterial and ______________ infections. Other medicines are meant to ______________ symptoms that cause discomfort. For example, though a throat lozenge will not cure a ______________ throat, the lozenge will make it more ______________ while your immune system does its work.

Preventive measures

balanced	hygiene	regular
contracting	prevention	system
hand	recovering	vaccinations

One proverb in English says that an ounce of ______________ is worth a pound of cure. In other words, it is better to spend a little time and energy to avoid getting sick than to spend a lot of time and energy ______________ after you are already sick. There are many things you can do to avoid ______________ an illness. The most important thing you can do is keep your immune ______________ healthy. Three things that will help with that are eating a ______________ diet, getting ______________ exercise, and reducing stress in your life. You can also get ______________ that will make you immune to many major illnesses. Finally, you can prevent germs from entering your body by maintaining a high level of personal ______________. This can include things such as frequent ______________ washing.

PUZZLE 7·4

Crossword: Disease and medicine

1, 2 C, 3, 4 N, L, 5 C, 6, 7 M, 8 F, 9 R, 10 R, 11, 12, 13 D, 14, 15, 16, 17 K, 18, 19, 20, 21 S, 22, 23, 24, 25 G, 26 C, 27, 28 P

Across

2. A substance used to immunize people.
4. Not harmful medically.
5. A ______ ailment is an ailment that comes back again and again.
6. Protected against catching a certain disease.
14. A person who seeks medical aid.
15. A ______ disease is a disease that can be spread from person to person.
16. Good medical advice: Get a second ______.
17. Something used to relieve pain.
19. A disease that spreads widely.
21. An organism such as a worm that lives inside another organism.
23. Another word for operation.
25. A medical term for germ.
26. A single-celled, disease-causing microbe.
27. A microorganism such as a virus or bacterium that causes disease.
28. A doctor that specializes in one type of disease.

Down

1. A microbe such as a mold that can cause disease.
2. A disease-causing microbe.
3. Another word for illness (usually mild or chronic).
5. A regular visit to a doctor to make sure you are healthy even when no symptoms are apparent.
7. A sign of an illness.
8. An invasion of your body by a disease-causing microbe.
9. Something your doctor gives you so you can get medicine.
10. The steps and medicines needed to cure a disease.
11. Medicines that kill living microbes such as bacteria or fungi.
12. An abnormal growth in your body that can be benign or malignant.
13. Any material that helps a patient fight disease or recover from an illness.
18. Another word for cure.
20. Heal an illness.
22. Get over an illness.
24. A family doctor: A ______ practitioner.

Word search: Disease and medicine *Find the following words in the grid.*

```
P T P W G E N E R A L P R A C T I T I O N E R K
J E Z T G X I T H P A I N K I L L E R C F D R W
Z I S C U O M U Y E A A C A S P E C I A L I S T
X V R I M J M M G B K R E X U T R E A T M E N T
D X K V I I U O I F A P A K P R E V E N T I O N
Y C X K W P N R E M M C C S G G S F U N G U S N
V I R U S R I F N D M E T F I P A T H O G E N S
G E R M S E Z N E O H U X E F T Z C U R E M W Z
H G U I N S A Y J C O M N V R R E G B N O R M K
L F O U Q C T Y T E T F B E N I G N I H X S O T
F C D H Y R I V A C C I N E S Z A C A S D X E S
A N T I B I O T I C S T O P S Y I C H R O N I C
M F S P J P N N M E O E I N A D S U R G E R Y R
A M M B L T S Y M P T O M O E T V T U Y I E U W
C U W R D I A G N O S I S M N N I R E L I E V E
L D O C T O R E M E D Y P L T F K E P M N W R T
R K T I U N B L O O D S A M P L E W N Q M G B O
E P I D E M I C O N T A G I O U S C K T L S D J
```

antibiotics
bacteria
benign
blood sample
checkup
chronic
contagious
cure
diagnosis
doctor
epidemic
fungus

general practitioner
germs
hygiene
immune system
immunization
infection
injection
lump
medicine
painkiller
parasite
pathogens

patient
prescription
prevention
relieve
remedy
specialist
surgery
symptom
treatment
tumor
vaccines
virus

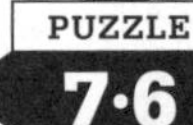

Word paths: Disease and medicine *Find and circle the secret words by following a connected path through the maze. Some words may overlap.*

G	L	R	G	E	A	U	C	C	U	G
E		U		R		R		H		H
R	M	S	T	Y	E	E	R	R	I	D
S		T		H		E		O		I
B	P	A	I	N	E	C	I	N	G	A
S		T		K		U		O		M
R	E	L	L	I	A	T	E	S	I	S
E		D		L		I		I		I
R	U	S	C	M	E	N	T	U	R	B
I		Y		O		F		I		N
V	N	M	P	T	E	E	C	T	I	O

1. A medicine that relieves pain. _ _ _ _ _ _ _ _ _ _
2. The type of pathogen responsible for colds. _ _ _ _ _
3. A doctor's determination of a disease. _ _ _ _ _ _ _ _ _
4. Purple or blue mark under the skin. _ _ _ _ _ _
5. A minor or chronic illness. _ _ _ _ _ _ _
6. An injury caused by a knife. _ _ _
7. A sign of an illness. _ _ _ _ _ _ _
8. (An illness that) returns from time to time. _ _ _ _ _ _ _
9. Another word for operation. _ _ _ _ _ _ _
10. Another word for heal. _ _ _ _
11. Microbes such as bacteria or viruses that cause diseases. _ _ _ _ _
12. A condition in which microbes enter your body and begin to grow. _ _ _ _ _ _ _

Hidden message: A good remedy *Use the remaining letters to uncover a phrase related to curing something.*

A good remedy:

_ _ _ _ _ _ _ _   _ _   _ _ _   _ _ _ _   _ _ _ _ _ _ _ _.

Psychology and mental disorders

VOCABULARY

abnormal	disorder	paranoia
abuse	empathy	perception
amnesia	guilt	phobia
anxiety	hallucination	psychologist
aversion	irrational	self-esteem
aware	insomnia	sensation
cope	intuition	sociopath/psychopath
counseling	mental	suppress
daydream	nightmare	treatment
delusion	obsession	unconscious
depression	panic attack	

PUZZLE 8·1

Definition match-up: Psychology and mental disorders *Match the following definitions with words from the vocabulary list. More than one word may fit some of the definitions.*

1. Unusual or deviant: ________________
2. Something you can't stop thinking about: ________________
3. The feeling that something is true even though you don't have proof: ________________
4. Deal with a problem or situation: ________________
5. An abnormal mental or physical condition: ________________
6. Mistreatment: ________________
7. Have knowledge of something: ________________
8. A feeling of something physical such as a sound or a sight: ________________
9. A sensation manufactured by the brain that is not real: ________________
10. Not allow yourself to feel an emotion: ________________
11. How you feel about yourself: ________________

12. Another word for psychological: ____________________

13. A person with an antisocial personality disorder: ____________________

14. A false belief despite evidence to the contrary: ____________________

PUZZLE **8·2**

Fill in the blanks: Context *Use the context to choose the correct word for the blank from the four choices given.*

1. He was under the ____________ that everyone would vote for him when in fact few people would.

   daydream delusion hallucination intuition

2. If you ____________ how you feel, you may eventually explode with anger.

   cope hallucinate suppress treat

3. She was ____________ that her coworkers were talking about her behind her back when in fact they never talked about her at all.

   aware paranoid perception phobia

4. ____________ often lack remorse or shame for harm they have caused other people.

   children counselors psychologists sociopaths

5. He was ____________ with his appearance and constantly looked at himself in the mirror.

   abnormal irrational obsessed suppressed

6. Her husband mentally ____________ her, ridiculing her constantly.

   abused disordered empathized illness

7. Her ____________ was so bad she couldn't even remember her own name.

   amnesia daydream depression hallucination

8. He could feel the anxiety building up and was worried that a ____________ attack was coming on.

   abnormal cope mental panic

9. She lacked ____________ and didn't care about the suffering around her.

   amnesia aversion empathy sensation

10. Although the ____________ seemed real, it was all in his head.

    amnesia guilt hallucination insomnia

11. He had low ____________ and was afraid to participate in the activities.

    insomnia intuition panic self-esteem

12. I can feel this strange ____________ of floating in water.

    delusion disorder illness sensation

PUZZLE 8·3

Labeling: Psychology and mental disorders *Attach the following psychology-related labels to the lists of words that follow.*

Instances of losing reality
Irrational fears or worries
Physical sensations
Treatments for mental disorders
Ways to understand the world
Words that mean "health problem"

1. delusions, hallucinations, paranoia ____________________
2. anxiety, panic, phobia ____________________
3. antidepressants, counseling, medication ____________________
4. condition, disorder, illness ____________________
5. touch, sight, sound ____________________
6. logic, reason, intuition ____________________

PUZZLE 8·4

Fill in the blanks: Psychology and mental disorders *Complete the following paragraphs by filling in the blanks using the words provided.*

Mental disorders

amnesia
causes
discrimination
disorder
insomnia
panic
paranoia
psychological
social

A mental ____________ is an abnormal ____________ condition that can seriously affect a person's life. Some examples of mental disorders include ____________, which is the inability to remember, and ____________, which is the inability to sleep. Some people with mental disorders suffer from ____________, which is a deep mistrust of other people. Still other people with mental disorders suffer from anxiety and have ____________ attacks. The ____________ of mental disorders are varied and often not well understood by scientists. Unfortunately, many people who suffer from mental disorders also suffer from ____________ stigmatization and ____________ as well.

Déjà vu

been
déjà vu
done
eerie
French
recognize
sensation
surroundings

Have you ever had the ____________ that you've ____________ somewhere or ____________ something before even though you know you haven't? This phenomenon of feeling like you've experienced something that you haven't is called ______________. It comes from ______________ and means "already seen." The opposite phenomenon is *jamais vu* which is the ______________ sensation of not being able to ______________ something that you rationally know you should recognize. For example, you might momentarily not recognize your ______________ even though you know you've been their before.

Hallucinations

affect	dementia	mind
common	fever	real
crawling	hallucinations	voices

______________ are sensations that seem ______________ but are in fact created by the ______________. They can ______________ any of your senses. You might for example feel something ______________ on your skin or see a light that isn't there. One of the most ______________ hallucinations is hearing ______________ when nobody is talking. Hallucinations have many causes including high ______________, psychiatric disorders such as schizophrenia, and ______________, which is the degeneration of the brain.

Phobias

claustrophobia	fear	spiders
confined	irrational	terrified
control	phobia	threat

A ______________ is an ______________ fear of something that causes a person to lose ______________. This fear is usually disproportionate to the ______________ posed by the object or situation that causes the fear. There are many different types of phobias. For example, some people are ______________ of being put in a narrow, ______________ space. This is called ______________. Other people have a ______________ of heights called acrophobia. Still others have arachnophobia and panic when they are near ______________.

Clinical depression

antidepressant	counseling	insomnia
blues	disorder	interest
clinical	disrupt	persistent

Everybody gets the ______________ from time to time. However, a ______________ low mood may be a symptom of ______________ depression, which is also known as major depressive ______________. This condition is a serious condition that can affect a person's general health and cause a sleeping disorder known as ______________. It can also seriously ______________ their work, school, and family life. This disorder is characterized by a loss of ______________ in activities that a person would normally find enjoyable. Typically, this disorder is treated with ______________ medications and ______________ by a psychotherapist.

Idiom puzzle: Mind-ful *Complete the following idioms. Use the symbols below the blanks to help you solve the idioms. Each symbol represents one letter.*

1. Amaze you: _ _ _ _ YOUR MIND
   ♥ ♦ 2
2. Go insane: _ _ _ _ YOUR MIND
   5 ♠ ★ ■
3. Decide to do something: _ _ _ _ UP YOUR MIND
   18 ♣ ■
4. In your imagination: IN YOUR MIND'S _ _ _
   ■ 9 ■
5. Cause you to stop worrying: PUT YOUR MIND AT _ _ _ _
   ■ ◐ 22 ■
6. Sane: IN YOUR _ _ _ _ _ MIND
   ▲ ▣ ♪ 20 23
7. Crazy: _ _ _ OF YOUR MIND
   ♠ 11 Δ
8. Forgetful: _ _ _ _ _ _-MINDED
   ◐ ♥ ★ 8 17 Δ
9. Many worries: A _ _ _ ON YOUR MIND
   ♦ 21 Δ
10. An optimistic mood: A _ _ _ _ _ _ _ _ FRAME OF MIND
    ▼ ♠ ★ ▣ Δ ▣ 12 ■
11. Stop thinking about something: _ _ _ _ YOUR MIND OFF IT
    Δ ◐ 4 ■
12. I forgot to do it: IT _ _ _ _ _ _ _ MY MIND
    ★ ♦ 6 ▼ ▼ ■ ∞
13. Guess what someone is thinking: _ _ _ _ THEIR MIND
    ▲ 16 ◐ ∞
14. Don't forget: _ _ _ _ IN MIND
    ♣ 13 ■ ▼
15. Perplexing or baffling: MIND-_ _ _ _ _ _ _ _
    ♥ 3 ♪ 19 ♦ ▣ Ω ♪
16. Say what you are thinking: _ _ _ _ _ YOUR MIND
    14 ▼ 15 ◐ ♣
17. I *did* think about it: IT _ _ _ _ _ _ _ MY MIND
    ▲ 10 ★ ★ ■ ∞
18. I suddenly forgot: MY MIND WENT _ _ _ _ _
    ♥ 1 ◐ Ω 7

PUZZLE 8·6

Code breaker *Use the number code in Puzzle 8•5 to solve the phrase.*

Appear shocked or frightened:

_ _ _ _   _ _ _ _   _ _ _'_ _   _ _ _ _   _   _ _ _ _ _

1 2 3 4   5 6 7 8   9 10 11 12 13   14 15 16 17   18   19 20 21 22 23

PUZZLE 8·7

Word paths: Psychology and the mind *Find and circle the secret words by following a connected path through the maze. Some words may overlap.*

G	A	N	O	B	S	E	S	S	I	O
Y	■	X	■	R	■	N	■	E	■	N
T	E	I	A	C	O	S	A	T	I	O
T	■	M	■	I	■	I	■	N	■	D
H	T	A	P	O	S	H	T	M	A	R
T	■	H	■	I	■	G	■	N	■	E
H	O	B	I	A	N	I	K	O	R	D
P	■	A	■	C	■	L	■	S	■	I
I	A	E	P	O	N	A	D	I	A	I
S	■	K	■	I	■	R	■	N	■	N
E	N	M	A	A	E	A	P	S	O	M

1. An uncontrollable, irrational fear. _ _ _ _ _ _
2. The inability to sleep. _ _ _ _ _ _ _ _
3. The inability to remember. _ _ _ _ _ _ _
4. A feeling of worry or unease. _ _ _ _ _ _ _
5. Deal with a problem or situation. _ _ _ _
6. A sight, sound, smell, taste, or feeling. _ _ _ _ _ _ _ _ _
7. Something you constantly think about. _ _ _ _ _ _ _ _ _
8. An irrational mistrust of others. _ _ _ _ _ _ _ _

9. A terrifying dream. __________

10. An abnormal mental condition. ________

11. A person with extreme antisocial behavior. __________

Hidden message: A problem idiom *Use the remaining letters to uncover an idiom related to feelings and emotions.*

Intelligent people come to the same conclusions.

_ _ _ _ _   _ _ _ _ _   _ _ _ _ _   _ _ _ _ _.

PUZZLE **8·8**

Word scramble: Psychology and mental disorders *Use the clues on the left to unscramble the letters and form words used to discuss psychology and mental disorders.*

Clue	Scrambled	Answer (numbered positions)
1. A terrifying dream:	GTHMRAENI	_ _ _ _ _ _ _ _ _ (18, 25)
2. Think pleasant thoughts that distract you:	MERADDAY	_ _ _ _ _ _ _ _ (4)
3. The ability to share the feelings of others:	PATEMYH	_ _ _ _ _ _ _ (10, 5)
4. Of the mind:	NMTLEA	_ _ _ _ _ _ (9, 28)
5. An irrational fear:	HOPIAB	_ _ _ _ _ _ (2, 12)
6. The refusal to admit an unpleasant truth:	NDELIA	_ _ _ _ _ _ (30, 1)
7. An abnormal mental condition:	ODRERSID	_ _ _ _ _ _ _ _ (17, 27)
8. Deal with a problem or bad situation:	PCOE	_ _ _ _ (16, 14)
9. Deep irrational mistrust of other people:	ARPNAAIO	_ _ _ _ _ _ _ _ (8, 6)
10. Mistreatment of someone:	SUBEA	_ _ _ _ _ (7, 15)
11. The inability to remember:	MEANAIS	_ _ _ _ _ _ _ (19, 29)
12. Nervousness or worry:	AXNITEY	_ _ _ _ _ _ _ (20, 22)
13. Stop yourself from feeling an emotion:	SPURESSP	_ _ _ _ _ _ _ _ (31, 24, 26)
14. A physical feeling or perception:	ATSENIONS	_ _ _ _ _ _ _ _ _ (3, 21)
15. Unusual or not regular:	NMROLABA	_ _ _ _ _ _ _ _ (23, 11, 13)

PUZZLE 8·9

Code breaker *Use the number code in Puzzle 8•8 to solve the idioms that are related to mental health.*

Idiom 1

Go insane:

__ __ __ __   __ __ __ __   __ __ __ __ __ __ __
1 2 3 4   5 6 7 8   9 10 11 12 13 14 15

Idiom 2

Start to think clearly again:

__ __ __ __   __ __   __ __ __ __   __ __ __ __ __ __
16 17 18 19   20 21   22 23 24 25   26 27 28 29 30 31

PUZZLE 8·10

Crossword: Psychology and the mind

Across

2. Psychological.
5. Not logical or reasonable.
7. Refusal to face an unpleasant truth.
8. An irrational, uncontrollable fear of something.
10. Intense fear or anxiety that prevents you from doing anything.
14. An irrational fear that other people are trying to harm you.
15. A sensation that is created by your mind.
18. A feeling of knowing or understanding without conscious reasoning.
19. How you view yourself.
20. The ability to share someone else's feelings.

Down

1. The ability to become aware of sensations.
3. Know of a fact or situation.
4. A physical feeling such as a touch, a sight, or a sound.
6. An abnormal mental or physical condition.
7. Extreme long-lasting unhappiness.
9. Not awake.
11. The inability to remember.
12. Sleeplessness.
13. Something that you constantly focus on.
16. Mistreatment.
17. Nervousness or worry.

Problems and solutions

·9·

VOCABULARY

adverse
alleviate
avert
brainstorm
burden
cost effective
crisis
desperate gamble
deteriorate
dilemma
drawback
extreme measures
feasible
fortify
futile
hinder
impact
impediment
last resort
mitigate
obstacle
obstruct
panacea
pragmatic
predicament
prevail
propose
prudent
scapegoat
setback
strengthen
stumbling block
sustainable

PUZZLE 9·1

Definition match-up: Problems and solutions *Match the following definitions with words from the vocabulary list. More than one word may fit some of the definitions.*

1. Get worse: ______________________
2. Hopeless: ______________________
3. Something in the way: ______________________
4. Wise: ______________________
5. A difficult choice: ______________________
6. The effect something has: ______________________
7. Can be maintained over time: ______________________
8. Practical, can be accomplished: ______________________
9. Come up with ideas: ______________________
10. Prevent a disaster from happening: ______________________
11. What you do when all else fails: ______________________
12. A cure for everything: ______________________
13. Strengthen: ______________________
14. A person who is unfairly blamed: ______________________

PUZZLE

9·2

Collocation match-up: Problems and solutions *Match the following words with their collocations.*

beyond	extreme	minor	underlying
cost	last	stumbling	worst-case

1. ____________ setback
2. ____________ resort
3. ____________ scenario
4. ____________ measures
5. ____________ block
6. ____________ effective
7. ____________ cause
8. ____________ hope

PUZZLE

9·3

Labeling: Problems and solutions *Attach the following labels to the lists of words that follow.*

Can't be solved	Make less severe	Solutions
Criteria for evaluating solutions	Prevent from doing	Things that get in the way
Fundamental reasons a problem occurs	Problem situations	What is done when all else fails

1. impediment, obstacle, stumbling block ____________
2. hamper, hinder, impede ____________
3. alleviate, ameliorate, mitigate ____________
4. crisis, dilemma, predicament ____________
5. cost effective, feasible, sustainable ____________
6. last resort, desperate gamble, extreme measures ____________
7. answer, remedy, panacea ____________
8. root cause, source, underlying cause ____________
9. beyond hope, futile, hopeless ____________

PUZZLE 9·4

Fill in the blanks: Problems and solutions *Complete the following paragraphs by filling in the blanks using the words provided.*

Dilemmas

consequences	Odysseus	sea monsters
dilemma	opted	undesirable
evils	risk	

Traditionally, a ______________ is a situation in which you have to choose between two ______________ courses of action. That is to say, you are trying to choose the lesser of two ______________. For example, the Greek hero ______________ had to sail his ship between two ______________: One monster would certainly kill a few of his men but not all of them. The other monster would either destroy the ship completely (killing everyone) or possibly let the ship pass unharmed. Odysseus ______________ to allow some of his men to die rather than ______________ all of his men dying. In modern usage, however, a dilemma has come to mean any difficult decision whether the ______________ of that decision are bad or not.

Identifying problems

biased	experts	multiple
case	gather	solutions
crisis	interviewing	underlying

When a ______________ arises, it is important to identify the ______________ causes before coming up with ______________. To accomplish this, you need to ______________ information. This may include ______________ people or asking for assessments from ______________. If that is the ______________, it is important to use ______________ sources of information because any one source may be ______________.

Coming up with solutions

brainstorm	matter	outside
evaluate	mind	perspective
ideas	mistake	potential

Once a problem has been identified, the next step is to ______________ and come up with ______________ solutions. When you brainstorm, you should write down on paper whatever ______________ you come up with no ______________ how bad the ideas may seem. You can cross them off later when you ______________ your solutions. Many people make the ______________ of trying to use the first solution that comes to ______________. Instead, you should try to think up as many possible solutions as you can. Try to think ______________ the box to come up with original solutions, and when you are done, ask others for advice to get some fresh ______________.

Evaluating solutions

come	effective	paper
consider	effort	sustainable
criteria	feasible	temporary

Once you have ____________ up with solutions, you need some ____________ to evaluate whether or not they are good solutions. Some solutions that look good on ____________ are not ____________ in reality. One thing to ____________ is if a solution is cost ____________. That is to say, is it really worth the money, time, and ____________ needed to solve the problem that way? Another thing to consider is whether or not the solution is ____________. In other words, will it solve the problem permanently, or is it just a ____________ fix?

Extreme measures

desperate	justifies	morally
fails	last	question
insurmountable	measures	risky

When problems seem ____________, people may resort to extreme ____________ to overcome them. When all else ____________, people may end up doing things as a ____________ resort that they wouldn't otherwise do. In a ____________ gamble, they may try something ____________. Or they may do something ____________ reprehensible. One ____________ to ask in these situations is whether or not the end ____________ the means. That is to say, is it okay to do anything so long as it solves the problem?

PUZZLE
9·5

Idiom puzzle: Problems and solutions *Complete the following idioms. Use the symbols below the blanks to help you solve the idioms. Each symbol represents one letter.*

1. Come up with ideas: _ _ _ _ _ _ _ _ _ _
   ▲ ♣ ◐ ▼ 17 ▣ ♥ 23 ♣ ★
2. Survive hardships: OVERCOME _ _ _ _ _ _ _ _ _
   ◐ ∑ ♪ ■ ♣ ▣ 26 ♥ 21
3. Need to make a difficult decision: HAVE A _ _ _ _ _ _ _
   ∑ 6 Δ ■ ★ ★ 28
4. A risky plan: A DESPERATE _ _ _ _ _ _
   ♠ 14 ★ ▲ Δ ■
5. Solve a problem: FIND A _ _ _ _ _ _ _ _
   ▣ Ω Δ ∞ 31 ▼ Ω 15
6. The solution to some dilemmas: THE _ _ _ _ _ _ OF TWO EVILS
   Δ ■ ▣ ▣ 11 ♣
7. Come up with a course of action: _ _ _ _ _ _ A PLAN
   ∑ ■ ♪ ▼ ▣ 3
8. Get data: _ _ _ _ _ _ INFORMATION
   ♠ ◐ ♥ 13 ■ 4
9. Another person's opinion: FRESH _ _ _ _ _ _ _ _ _ _ _
   ● ■ ♣ ▣ ● ■ 29 12 ▼ ♪ ■
10. Reduce the harm caused: _ _ _ _ _ _ _ _ THE DAMAGE
    8 ▼ ♥ ▼ ♠ 30 ♥ ■
11. Do something drastic: TAKE EXTREME _ _ _ _ _ _ _ _
    ★ ■ 20 ▣ ∞ ♣ ■ 7
12. If all goes wrong: _ _ _ _ _-_ _ _ _ SCENARIO
    19 Ω 10 ▣ ♥ ♦ ◐ ▣ ■
13. The real reason something happened: THE UNDERLYING _ _ _ _ _
    ♦ ◐ ∞ 24 18
14. An action for when all else fails: A LAST _ _ _ _ _ _
    ♣ 5 ▣ Ω ♣ 22
15. No matter what: AT ALL _ _ _ _ _
    ♦ 9 ▣ ♥ ▣
16. A predicament: A STICKY _ _ _ _ _ _ _ _ _
    ▣ ▼ 1 ∞ ◐ ♥ ▼ Ω 27
17. An obstacle or impediment: A STUMBLING _ _ _ _ _
    ▲ Δ 16 ♦ 25
18. Futile: BEYOND _ _ _ _
    2 Ω ● ■

PUZZLE **9·6**

Code breaker: A proverb about problem solving *Use the number code in Puzzle 9•5 to solve the proverb.*

A problem may have many solutions.

_ _ _ _ _   _ _   _ _ _ _   _ _ _ _   _ _ _   _ _ _   _ _
1 2 3 4 5   6 7   8 9 10 11   12 13 14 15   16 17 18   19 20 21   22 23

_ _ _ _   _   _ _ _.
24 25 26 27   28   29 30 31

PUZZLE **9·7**

Word paths: Problem solving *Find and circle the secret words by following a connected path through the maze. Some words may overlap.*

A	N	A	C	E	D	R	E	S	I	S
P		I		A		U		I		G
R	A	T	M	E	A	S	C	R	Y	I
O		E		O		U		R		M
I	O	G	E	P	W	A	I	L	N	P
R		O		A		V		E		A
E	G	A	S	C	L	E	S	S	R	C
T		T		A		R		A		T
E	D	B	S	T	V	P	R	E	A	M
L		O		N		E		D		M
I	T	U	F	E	M	A	C	I	L	E

1. A troubling situation. ____________
2. Something in your way. _________
3. Hopeless. _______
4. Overcome hardship. ________
5. A person who is unfairly blamed. __________
6. Get worse. ____________
7. A hard choice. ________

8. A cure-all. _ _ _ _ _ _ _

9. Actions taken to solve a problem. _ _ _ _ _ _ _ _

10. A serious problem. _ _ _ _ _ _

11. Which evil you choose in a dilemma. _ _ _ _ _ _

12. The effect that something has. _ _ _ _ _ _

Hidden message: A problem idiom *Use the remaining letters to uncover an idiom related to feelings and emotions.*

Cause your own problems:

_ _ _   _ _ _ _   _ _ _   _ _ _ _ _

PUZZLE **9·8**

Word scramble: Problems and solutions *Use the clues on the left to unscramble the letters and form words used to discuss problems and solutions.*

Clue	Letters	Answer	Numbered letters
1. The answer to your problems:	U T S L O O N I	_ _ _ _ _ _ _ _	3, 13
2. A difficult choice:	M I D A L E M	_ _ _ _ _ _ _	26, 28
3. A stumbling block:	C L O B A T S E	_ _ _ _ _ _ _ _	16, 19
4. Fortify:	N E T H S R T N E G	_ _ _ _ _ _ _ _ _ _	12, 23
5. A dangerous situation:	S S C R I I	_ _ _ _ _ _	1, 25
6. Overcome adversity:	V A I L P R E	_ _ _ _ _ _ _	27, 2
7. Impede or hamper:	D I N H E R	_ _ _ _ _ _	5, 21
8. Can be accomplished:	E A F I S L E B	_ _ _ _ _ _ _ _	11, 31
9. Write down as many ideas as you can:	S T B R O R A I N M	_ _ _ _ _ _ _ _ _ _	7, 22
10. Your backup plan when all else fails:	S T L A E T R S O R	_ _ _ _ _ _ _ _ _ _	29, 6
11. A remedy for all your ailments:	C E A P A N A	_ _ _ _ _ _ _	17, 8
12. The effect your actions have:	M I P T A C	_ _ _ _ _ _	14, 30
13. A sticky situation:	D I C A P R E N E M T	_ _ _ _ _ _ _ _ _ _ _	15, 9
14. Someone who gets blamed unfairly:	C O A T S G A P E	_ _ _ _ _ _ _ _ _	24, 4
15. Deteriorate:	O R W N E S	_ _ _ _ _ _	10, 20
16. The opposite of benefit:	B R A C K D W A	_ _ _ _ _ _ _ _	18

PUZZLE 9·9

Code breaker *Use the number code in Puzzle 9•8 to solve the idiom that is related to problems.*

Trapped in a dilemma:

__ __ __ __ __ __   __ __ __ __ __ __ __   __   __ __ __ __   __ __ __   __
1 2 3 4 5 6   7 8 9 10 11 12 13   14   15 16 17 18   19 20 21   22

__ __ __ __   __ __ __ __ __
23 24 25 26   27 28 29 30 31

PUZZLE 9·10

Crossword: Problem solving

Across

2. A lost cause: ______ hope.
5. A remedy for all of your troubles.
8. Problem proverb: Kill two ______ with one stone.
10. The answer to your problem.
11. What you do when all else fails: your last ______.
13. Get worse.
14. A dilemma: Caught between the ______ and the deep blue sea.
15. A difficult choice.
17. Actions you take to solve or prevent a problem.
19. Practical. Can be done.
20. A dilemma: Caught between a ______ and a hard place.
22. An impediment.
24. A troubling situation.
26. The real reason a problem arises: The ______ cause.

Down

1. Cause trouble for yourself: Dig your own ______.
2. Come up with ideas.
3. Hopeless.
4. Hamper or impede.
6. The least bad choice: The lesser of two ______.
7. Reduce the damage or harm.
9. ______ a problem.
12. Be creative: Think ______ the box.
16. The effect that an action has.
18. Actions you take when you are desperate: ______ measures.
21. Worth the time, money, and effort: ______ effective.
23. ______ up with ideas.
25. Problem proverb: There is more than one way to skin a ______.

Technology and innovation

VOCABULARY

advanced	feature	obsolete
augment	foster	original
breakthrough	gadget	patent
component	groundbreaking	prototype
conceive	hybrid	state-of-the-art
copyright	innovation	stifle
creativity	inspire	trademark
cutting-edge	intellectual property	unique
develop	invention	visionary
device	modify	
entrepreneur	novel	

PUZZLE

Definition match-up: Technology and innovation *Match the following definitions with words from the vocabulary list. More than one word may fit some of the definitions.*

1. Legal protection for your brand name: ____________________
2. Legal protection for artistic works: ____________________
3. Legal protection for inventions: ____________________
4. Old-fashioned/out-of-date: ____________________
5. A part of a device or machine: ____________________
6. Change: ____________________
7. A small electronic device: ____________________
8. A businessperson who takes risks: ____________________
9. Something made by combining two elements: ____________________
10. Innovative or revolutionary: ____________________
11. Think of an idea: ____________________
12. Add to something to make it better: ____________________
13. Able to see the future before others: ____________________

14. Encourage or stimulate: ________________________

15. One of a kind/unusual: ________________________

16. New/never been done before: ________________________

PUZZLE **10·2**

Collocation match-up: Technology and innovation *Match the following words with their collocations below.*

added	bells	digital	product
advances	computer	intellectual	technological

1. ______________ property rights
2. ______________ breakthrough
3. ______________ life cycle
4. ______________ in technology
5. ______________ literate
6. ______________ features
7. ______________ and whistles
8. ______________ cameras

PUZZLE **10·3**

Labeling: Technology and innovation *Attach the following labels to the lists of words below.*

Adjectives used to describe advanced technologies
Intellectual property rights
Machines or tools
New technologies
Parts of something
People involved in developing new technologies
Words that mean "change"
Words that mean "create"
Words used to describe old technologies

1. design, develop, devise, generate, fabricate, produce ________________________
2. cutting-edge, groundbreaking, state-of-the-art ________________________
3. contraptions, devices, gadgets ________________________
4. copyright, patent, trademark ________________________
5. adapt, alter, augment, modify, revamp, tweak ________________________
6. innovations, inventions, technological breakthroughs ________________________
7. entrepreneurs, inventors, engineers ________________________
8. obsolete, old-fashioned, out-of-date ________________________
9. components, features, modules ________________________

PUZZLE 10·4

Fill in the blanks: Technology and innovation *Complete the paragraphs by filling in the blanks using the following words.*

Technology

agricultural	life span	revolutionized
history	printing	technologies
information	process	vaccinations

Throughout the course of ______________, humans have constantly created and implemented new ______________. Some of these technologies have ______________ society. For example, medical technologies such as ______________ have greatly increased our average ______________. Technologies such as the ______________ for manufacturing chemical fertilizers have vastly increased the world's ______________ output. The ______________ press raised literacy rates and improved our ability to store and retrieve ______________.

Technology and the product life cycle

art	down	prices
consumer	edge	products
cycle	obsolete	replaced

When ______________ goods using advanced technology first hit the market, they are said to be state-of-the-______________. Companies that create new technologies can often command high ______________ when their ______________ first reach the market. Eventually however, competitors will copy their success and drive the price ______________. As well, new technologies are constantly developed so that today's cutting-______________ technology will be ______________ by even more advanced technologies and become ______________ in the future. This is all part of a product's life ______________.

Modifying old technologies

access	features	materials
augmenting	innovations	modified
existing	lightweight	performance

Many of the most important ______________ in technology are not new inventions but are instead improvements of ______________ technology. One way that old technologies can be ______________ is by ______________ them with new ______________. Smartphones, for example, are phones that can ______________ the Internet. Another way that old technologies can be altered is by changing the ______________ used to make things. New sturdy, ______________ metal alloys vastly improve the ______________ of cars and airplanes.

Drawbacks of technology

deforming	durable	point
detrimental	materials	widespread
drawbacks	pesticides	

There is no denying that the ______________ use of technology has benefited humans. However, many technologies come with significant ______________ as well. Many technologies have had a ______________ impact on the environment, for example. The invention of plastic is a case in ______________. Plastic, which is cheap, lightweight, and ______________, is one of the most versatile ______________ in existence. However, plastic ends up floating in the ocean and killing animals that eat it by mistake. Similarly, ______________ greatly improve our ability to grow crops, but they also work their way into the food chain, ______________ and killing animals.

Intellectual property rights

copyright	intellectual	period
exclusive	invention	rewarded
incentive	patent	

Most people who create and innovate expect to be ______________ for their effort. ______________ property rights are one way to ensure that people have ______________ to invent new technologies or create new works of art by giving creative individuals ______________ rights to profit from their work. A ______________ gives an inventor the sole right to use that ______________ for a set ______________ of time. A ______________ gives an artist or writer the sole right to make copies of his or her works.

PUZZLE

10·5

Idiom puzzle: Technology and innovation *Complete the following idioms. Use the symbols below the blanks to help you solve the idioms. Each symbol represents one letter.*

1. Prepare your computer for use: INSTALL A _ _ _ _ _ _ _
   ■ 27 ♦ 1 ♠ ♥ 32
2. Use the Internet: GO _ _ _ _ _ _
   2 ♣ ▼ ▣ ♣ ★
3. Made better: NEW AND _ _ _ _ _ _ _ _
   16 ♪ ■ 22 20 ◐ ★ ●
4. Get rid of something on your hard drive: _ _ _ _ _ _ A FILE
   ● ★ ▼ ★ 9 ★
5. Extra functions: ADDED _ _ _ _ _ _ _ _
   29 ★ 36 ▲ 13 ★ 24
6. Brainstorm: COME UP WITH _ _ _ _ _
   ▣ ● 11 26 Ω
7. Much more advanced than the competition: LIGHT-YEARS _ _ _ _ _
   ♥ 10 ★ ♥ 23
8. Good at using electronic devices: TECH _ _ _ _ _
   33 14 ◐ ◐
9. Knows how to use software: COMPUTER _ _ _ _ _ _ _ _
   ▼ ▣ ▲ ★ 30 ♥ 37 ★
10. Computers, websites, and the Internet: _ _ _ _ _ _ _ _ _ _ _ TECHNOLOGY
    ▣ ♣ 8 ♠ ♪ 21 28 ▣ ♦ ♣
11. What you use to find information: SEARCH _ _ _ _ _ _
    ★ ♣ 18 ▣ ♣ ★
12. The ability to go online: INTERNET _ _ _ _ _ _
    4 34 Δ ★ Ω Ω
13. Nonessential added features: _ _ _ _ _ AND WHISTLES
    19 ★ ▼ ▼ Ω
14. A way to access the Internet without a cable: WIRELESS _ _ _ _ _ _ _ _ _ _
    5 31 ♣ 17 ★ Δ ▲ ▣ ♦ ♣
15. A machine that helps us do work: LABOR-SAVING _ _ _ _ _ _
    12 ★ ◐ ▣ 38 ★
16. Easy to understand: NOT _ _ _ _ _ _ SCIENCE
    35 ♦ Δ 6 ★ 25
17. Advanced electronics: HIGH _ _ _ _
    7 ★ Δ 39
18. The Internet: WORLD WIDE _ _ _
    15 ★ 3

PUZZLE 10·6

Code breaker *Use the number code in Puzzle 10•5 to solve the two idioms about design.*

Begin designing from the absolute beginning:

Idiom 1

1 2   3 4 5 6   7 8   9 10 11   12 13 14 15 16 17 18   19 20 21 22 23

Idiom 2

24 25 26 27 28   29 30 31 32   33 34 35 36 37 38 39

PUZZLE 10·7

Word paths: Technology and innovation *Find and circle the secret words by following a connected path through the maze. Some words may overlap.*

C	U	T	R	S	O	L	E	E	N	T
I		T		B		E		T		H
G	N	I	D	O	M	T	P	A	N	Y
E		F		V		E		E		B
D	E	Y	T	O	T	O	N	C	T	R
G		P		T		R		I		I
E	H	E	E	N	O	P	W	V	E	D
T		C		E		M		H		E
H	E	O	T	N	C	O	N	N	V	E
G		P		O		V		I		N
I	R	Y	L	I	T	A	N	O	I	T

1. A new machine or product. _ _ _ _ _ _ _ _ _

2. State-of-the-art. _ _ _ _ _ _ _ - _ _ _ _

3. An improvement of a technology. _ _ _ _ _ _ _ _ _ _

4. An early version of a machine. _ _ _ _ _ _ _ _ _

5. Legal protection for an invention. _ _ _ _ _ _

6. A combination of two things. _ _ _ _ _ _

7. No longer used. _ _ _ _ _ _ _ _

8. A part of a machine _ _ _ _ _ _ _ _ _

9. Make a change. _ _ _ _ _ _

10. A machine, tool, or gadget. _ _ _ _ _ _

11. Legal protection for a written work. _ _ _ _ _ _ _ _ _

Hidden message: An idiom related to technology *Use the remaining letters to uncover an idiom related to technology.*

Waste effort doing something that's already been done:

_ _ _ _ _ _ _ _ _   _ _ _   _ _ _ _ _

Crossword: Technology and innovation

Across

1. Make or create.
5. A plan for making a machine.
6. Something made from two different things.
7. Get rid of a file.
8. Add to something to make it better.
9. Go online: _______ the Internet.
11. Think of an idea.
14. Can be used without cables or cords.
15. Load a program onto your computer.
17. New or original.

Down

1. An electronic or mechanical machine.
2. Has been replaced by more advanced technology.
3. Copyrights, patents, and trademarks: _______ property.
4. An improvement on existing technology.
10. Thinking that's outside the box.
12. A part of a machine or a device.
13. Made better.
16. An early model of a machine.
19. Advanced: cutting-_______.

Across

18. A new machine.
20. Legal protection for an artistic work.
22. Legal protection for an invention.
23. A property or function of an electronic device.

Down

21. Advanced: state-of-the-______.

PUZZLE

10·9

Word scramble: Technology and innovation *Use the clues on the left to unscramble the letters and form words used to discuss problems and solutions.*

1.	An improvement in a technology:	V A T N N I O N I O	__ __ __ __ __ __ __ __ __ __ (7, 25)
2.	A machine or tool:	V I C E D E	__ __ __ __ __ __ (19, 23)
3.	A small electronic device:	A D G T E G	__ __ __ __ __ __ (26, 12)
4.	Make something new:	R E T A E C	__ __ __ __ __ __ (3)
5.	The right to use an invention:	T A P N E T	__ __ __ __ __ __ (1, 28)
6.	Not useful anymore:	L E T E S O O B	__ __ __ __ __ __ __ __ (6, 17)
7.	An early model of an invention:	T O P O T R Y E P	__ __ __ __ __ __ __ __ __ (8, 30)
8.	A part of a machine:	C E N T O M P O N	__ __ __ __ __ __ __ __ __ (16, 31)
9.	An ability or function of a machine:	T E A F R U E	__ __ __ __ __ __ __ (22, 4)
10.	Think of an idea:	C O C E N I V E	__ __ __ __ __ __ __ __ (27, 14)
11.	Alter or change:	D O F I M Y	__ __ __ __ __ __ (15, 9)
12.	Something made by combining two things:	D R I B H Y	__ __ __ __ __ __ (13, 20)
13.	Advanced:	G H I H C H E T	__ __ __ __ __ __ __ __ (18, 29)
14.	New:	O V L E N	__ __ __ __ __ (21, 2)
15.	Something that causes you to be creative:	I N P I R S T I O N A	__ __ __ __ __ __ __ __ __ __ __ (10, 5)
16.	The plan for a machine:	E G D I S N	__ __ __ __ __ __ (11, 24)

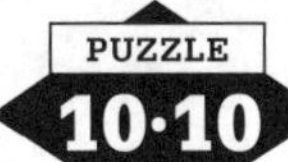

Code breaker *Use the number code in Puzzle 10•9 to solve the proverb below that is related to technology creation.*

The thing that inspires people to create:

__ __ __ __ __ __ __ __ __   __ __   __ __ __   __ __ __ __ __ __   __ __

1 2 3 4 5 6 7 8 9   10 11   12 13 14   15 16 17 18 19 20   21 22

__ __ __ __ __ __ __ __ __

23 24 25 26 27 28 29 30 31

History and civilization ·11·

VOCABULARY

agriculture
aqueduct
arable
archeology (also spelled *archaeology*)
architecture
artifact
artisan
barter
circa
civilization
clan
colony
conquer
currency
domestication
dynasty
era
exploration
irrigation
literacy
monument
mythology
navigation
nomad
oral tradition
pottery
remains
ruins
scribe
settlement
surplus
transmit

Definition match-up: History and civilization *Match the following definitions with words from the vocabulary list. More than one word may fit some of the definitions.*

1. The growing of crops: ____________
2. A system of canals, reservoirs, and dykes used to water crops: ____________
3. Can be farmed: ____________
4. The passing of stories and knowledge through spoken word: ____________
5. A person without a fixed home: ____________
6. A small group of humans usually based on kinship ties: ____________
7. The study of human remains and artifacts: ____________
8. The science of designing buildings: ____________
9. Trade goods without using money: ____________
10. A place where people build homes and live for long periods of time: ____________

11. A collection of stories about gods, heroes, and nature: ____________________

12. The science of knowing where you are and following routes: ____________________

13. The process of taming wild animals to raise for food: ____________________

14. A great work of architecture such as a pyramid or statue: ____________________

PUZZLE 11·2

Labeling: History and civilization *Attach the following labels to the lists of words below.*

Ancient civilizations
Locations of ancient civilizations
Metallurgy
Monumental architecture
Organized religion
People who study the past
Prehistoric periods
Social stratification
Systems of writing

1. bronze working, iron working, jewelry production ____________________
2. archeologists, historians, paleontologists ____________________
3. Egyptian, Minoan, Sumerian ____________________
4. alphabet, cuneiform, hieroglyphics ____________________
5. Indus Valley, Nile River, Fertile Crescent ____________________
6. Ice Age, Neolithic/New Stone Age, Paleolithic/Old Stone Age ____________________
7. pyramids, statues, ziggurats ____________________
8. monks, priests, temples ____________________
9. nobility, peasants, serfs, slaves ____________________

PUZZLE 11·3

Word sort: Historical collocations *Match the following words with their collocations below.*

Age of Exploration	explorer	Reformation
aristocrat	Industrial Revoluation	Renaissance
artisan	Iron Age	scribe
Bronze Age	Middle Ages	slave
emperor	monk	
Enlightenment	peasant	

HISTORICAL PEOPLE		HISTORICAL ERAS	
______	______	______	______
______	______	______	______
______	______	______	______
______	______	______	______

PUZZLE 11·4

Fill in the blanks: History and civilization *Complete the following paragraphs by filling in the blanks using the words provided.*

Early peoples

ancestors	bone	nomadic
archeologists	clans	writing
artifacts	gatherers	

Our early ____________ were hunter-____________ who lived a ____________ lifestyle, roaming around in search of food. They probably lived in small kinship groups called ____________ or tribes. Although they had not developed a system of ____________, they did create artworks on cave walls and tools made from stone, ____________, and wood. ____________ are scientists who study these ____________ left behind by early people.

Agriculture

agriculture	fertile	settle
civilizations	floods	surplus
ditches	irrigation	valleys

Many of the earliest ______________ began in river ______________. The development of ______________, which is the growing of crops, allowed people to give up their nomadic existence and ______________ down in one place. Rivers were an important source of water for ______________ works such as canals, ______________, and reservoirs. As well, yearly ______________ brought silt over the land, making rich, ______________ soil for farming. The growing of crops in turn led to a ______________ of food and population growth.

Hierarchical societies

aristocrats	hierachical	slavery
artisans	pottery	spread
chiefs	privileges	status

As agriculture ______________, the need for everyone to engage in food production decreased. A surplus of crops meant that some people were now free to specialize and become ______________ who could produce a range of goods from ______________ to weapons made from metal. Early societies also became more ______________ with some members enjoying ______________ and freedoms that others didn't have. Although some members of early societies such as ______________ and shamans enjoyed special ______________, inequality expanded greatly as cities developed and the first kings, priests, and ______________ appeared. As well, humans began depriving other humans of freedom and forcing them into ______________.

Early technologies

ability	migration	survive
bone	significance	technology
characteristics	skins	ward

One of the defining ______________ of the human species is the widespread use of tools and ______________. The ______________ to make and use fire gave humans a powerful weapon to ______________ off wild animals as well as a means of staying warm. Though most people know the ______________ of fire in human development, few people realize the importance of a very simple technology, the ______________ needle. Using needles, early humans could create formfitting clothes from animal ______________ that allowed them to ______________ in the harshest climates on earth. Without the needle, early human ______________ to the Americas might have been impossible.

The development of writing

achievements	literacy	spoken
affordable	printing	tradition
generation	scribes	

Perhaps one of the greatest human ______________ was the development of writing. Before writing was developed, culture and knowledge could only be passed down from ______________ to generation via the ______________ word in a process called oral ______________. But even after writing developed, ______________ was not widespread as the cost of producing written works was enormous. In many societies, only elite groups such as priests or ______________ could read. It was only after paper and the ______________ press were developed that written works became ______________ for many people.

PUZZLE **11·5**

Keyword clues: Historical eras and events *Use the keywords to identify the historical era or event. The Greek mythology clues that follow the puzzle can help you solve the historical era clues.*

1. _ _ _ _ _ _ _ _ _ _ _ (24 4) — Italian, realism, perspective drawing, art, Michelangelo, rebirth

2. _ _ _ _ _   _ _ _ _ _ _ _ _ _ _ (15 23 8) — economic downturn, unemployment, stock market crash, New Deal

3. _ _ _ _ _ _ _ _ _ _ _ _ _ (11 25) — Age of Reason, scientific method, religious toleration, intellectuals

4. _ _ _ _ _ _ _ _ _ _   _ _ _ _ _ _ _ _ _ _ (14 6 32) — machines, factories, child labor, mass production, coal, steel

5. _ _ _ _ _   _ _ _ _ _   _ _ _ (17 19 1) — machine guns, barbed wire, trench warfare, poison gas

6. _ _ _ _   _ _ _ _ (26 20 9) — strike it rich, boom towns, shovels, pickaxes, miners, mineshafts, claim

7. __ __ __ __ __ __ __ __ __ __
31 28

tin, copper, alloy, ancient civilizations, metallurgy, spears, jewelry

8. __ __ __ __ __ __ __
21 16

espionage, the Iron Curtain, nuclear arms race, spies, proxy war

9. __ __ __ __ __ __ __ __ __ __ __ __ __ __ __ __ __ __
29 12

North and South, United States, rebels, slavery, emancipation

10. __ __ __ __ __ __ __ __ __ __ __
2 22

plague, rats, spread, high mortality, outbreak, contagious, epidemic, buboes

11. __ __ __ __ __ __ __ __ __ __ __ __ __ __ __ __ __
3 27 18

guillotine, overthrow, monarchy, republic, Reign of Terror, Napoleon, France

12. __ __ __ __ __ __ __ __ __ __ __ __ __ __ __ __
10 33 5

navigation, caravel, voyage, map, discovery, contact, compass

13. __ __ __ __ __ __ __ __ __ __ __
13 7 30

knights, castles, lords, manors, serfdom, feudalism, vassals, armor, shields

Clues: Greek myths *The clues can help you solve the puzzle above.*

Clue 1: A person's fatal weakness: __ __ __ __ __ __ __ __' __ __ __ __
1 2 3 4 5 6 7 8 9 10 11 12

Clue 2: An ability to make money: __ __ __ __ __ __ __ __ __ __
13 14 15 16 17 18 19 20 21 22

Clue 3: A potential source of troubles: __ __ __ __ __ __ __' __ __ __ __
23 24 25 26 27 28 29 30 31 32 33

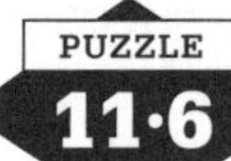

Word paths: Human history

Find and circle the secret words by following a connected path through the maze. Some words may overlap.

G	A	T	U	R	A	B	C	I	R	C
R		L		E		A		R		A
I	C	U	S	T	P	R	T	E	M	Y
A		R		C		T		N		T
O	M	A	D	A	F	I	S	A	T	H
N		A		N		E		Y		O
U	I	N	X	V	A	L	S	G	O	L
R		S		E		I		S		S
C	H	E	T	D	Y	N	E	U	L	P
R		O		N		A		C		R
A	E	L	O	G	I	S	T	Y	S	U

1. A person who digs up ancient civilizations (variant spelling). _ _ _ _ _ _ _ _ _ _ _ _
2. Trade goods without using money. _ _ _ _ _ _
3. Something made by humans. _ _ _ _ _ _ _ _
4. A person who wanders. _ _ _ _ _
5. A person who is not free. _ _ _ _ _
6. A person who specializes in making things. _ _ _ _ _ _ _
7. A line of rulers from the same family. _ _ _ _ _ _ _
8. The remains of a long lost civilization. _ _ _ _ _
9. Extra of something. _ _ _ _ _ _ _
10. The growing of crops. _ _ _ _ _ _ _ _ _ _ _
11. Around the time of. _ _ _ _ _
12. A collection of stories about gods and heroes. _ _ _ _ _ _ _ _ _

Hidden message: A historical idiom *Use the remaining letters to uncover an idiom from history.*

A life without luxury or comfort:

_ _

Crossword: Human history

Across

2. Invade and control another civilization.
6. The remains of a destroyed city.
8. Something made by humans.
9. Alphabet, cuneiform, or hieroglyphics: systems of ______.
10. A person who makes things by hand.
13. A system for watering crops.

Down

1. A person who digs up ancient civilizations.
2. Around the time of.
3. Passing down knowledge through spoken word: ______ tradition.
4. An advanced society.
5. The science of finding your location.
7. A person who could write.

Across

14. The process of taming and raising animals.
16. A person who wanders around.
19. An extra amount of something.
21. A metal alloy made from tin and copper.
22. The ability to read and write.

Down

10. The growing of crops.
11. The exchange of goods between civilizations.
12. Things left behind.
15. Exchange goods for other goods without using money.
17. A story about gods or heroes.
18. A series of kings or queens from one family.
20. A person who is not free.

Word scramble: History and civilization

Use the clues on the left to unscramble the letters and form words used to discuss history and civilization.

Clue	Scrambled	Answer
1. A collection of stories and legends:	L O M T H Y Y G O	_ _ _ _ _ _ _ _ _ (3, 21, 27)
2. Trade goods for goods:	T A R B R E	_ _ _ _ _ _ (9, 38)
3. The destroyed remains of a city:	N U I R S	_ _ _ _ _ (26, 15, 23)
4. The growing of crops:	G R I A T U R E C U L	_ _ _ _ _ _ _ _ _ _ _ (32, 11, 24)
5. Roman, Greek, Egyptian, or Persian:	C I A T I O N V I L I Z	_ _ _ _ _ _ _ _ _ _ _ _ (39, 12, 25)
6. Something made by human hands:	F A C A R T T I	_ _ _ _ _ _ _ _ (1, 36, 40, 14)
7. A person who came before you:	C E S A N T O R	_ _ _ _ _ _ _ _ (31, 34, 2)
8. Around that time:	I R C A C	_ _ _ _ _ (35, 6)
9. A system for watering crops:	T I O N I R R A G I	_ _ _ _ _ _ _ _ _ _ (28, 19)
10. A series of rulers from a single family:	A S T Y D Y N	_ _ _ _ _ _ _ (18, 16, 20)
11. A historic era:	G E A	_ _ _ (17, 29)
12. A metal alloy made from tin and copper:	O N Z R B E	_ _ _ _ _ _ (10, 8)

13. Pyramids, statues, and other works: M O N N E M T U S __ __ __ __ __ __ __ __ __ (4, 33)

14. What scribes do: R I T E W __ __ __ __ __ (5, 22)

15. An extra amount of something: P U L S S U R __ __ __ __ __ __ __ (7, 30 13, 37)

PUZZLE 11·9

Code breaker: History-related proverbs *Use the number code in Puzzle 11•8 to solve the history-related proverbs.*

Proverb 1

Things take time.

__ __ __ __   __ __ __ __'__   __ __ __ __ __   __ __   __   __ __ __.

1 2 3 4   5 6 7 8 9   10 11 12 13 14   15 16   17   18 19 20

Proverb 2

The same things happen over and over again.

__ __ __ __ __ __ __   __ __ __ __ __ __ __   __ __ __ __ __ __.

21 22 23 24 25 26 27   28 29 30 31 32 33 34   35 36 37 38 39 40

Banking and personal finance

VOCABULARY

assets	deposit	return
balance	diversify	risk
bonds	funds	savings
budget	insurance	speculate
cash	interest	statement
checking	investment	shares/stocks
collateral	loan	teller
credit card	mortgage	term
credit check	payee	transaction
debit card	payment	withdraw
debt	pension	

PUZZLE **12·1**

Definition match-up: Banking and personal finance *Match the following definitions with words from the vocabulary list. More than one word may fit some of the definitions.*

1. Put money into a bank account: ____________________
2. Take money out of a bank account: ____________________
3. Any exchange of money, goods, or services: ____________________
4. Money owed to someone: ____________________
5. How much money you have in your account: ____________________
6. A monthly written record of your bank balance: ____________________
7. A bank loan that is used to buy a house: ____________________
8. The cost of borrowing money from the bank: ____________________
9. Things of value that you own: ____________________
10. A financial instrument that pays compensation in case of loss, damage, or death: ____________________
11. A person who works at a bank: ____________________
12. Money you receive after you retire: ____________________

13. Another word for money (cash or electronic): ______________________

14. Paper money or coins: ______________________

15. The purchase of something (like stocks or bonds) in the hope of getting future profits: ______________________

16. Investments that give you part ownership of a company: ______________________

17. Investments that usually give you a fixed return: ______________________

18. The chance that an investment will lose money: ______________________

19. A bank account that you use for daily transactions: ______________________

20. A bank account you put money into and leave it there to accrue interest: ______________________

PUZZLE **12·2**

Collocation match-up: Part 1 *Match the following banking words with their collocations.*

diversify	insurance	stocks
housing	return	transaction

1. ____________ and bonds
2. ____________ on investment
3. ____________ policy
4. ____________ fees
5. ____________ your risks
6. ____________ market

PUZZLE **12·3**

Fill in the blanks: Banking and personal finance *Complete the following paragraphs by filling in the blanks using the words provided.*

Bank accounts

checking	interest	transaction
debit	robbed	withdraw
deposit	savings	
fire	sums	

Keeping large ____________ of money inside your home is dangerous. Your home may be ____________ by a burglar or destroyed in a ____________, in which case you would lose everything. On top of that, your money doesn't earn anything sitting at home. Therefore, most people ____________ their extra money into a bank account. Two common accounts are ______________ accounts and ______________ accounts. Savings accounts usually pay higher ______________, but checking accounts usually have fewer ______________ fees so most people use checking accounts for their day-to-day transactions. Another advantage of having a bank account nowadays is that most banks give you a ______________ card so you can ______________ your funds whenever and wherever you want.

Buying a house

afford	funds	payment
credit	market	percent
estate	mortgage	purchase

A home is the most expensive ______________ that many people make in their lives. Few people can ______________ to buy a home with ______________ from their bank account. Instead, most people have to take out a special housing loan called a ______________. To get a mortgage, most banks require that you have enough money for a down ______________. This is typically between ten and twenty ______________ of the cost of the home. The bank will also do a ______________ evaluation to make sure you will be able to pay off your mortgage. Once you have secured financing, you need to look at what is available on the housing ______________. To do this, most people contact a real ______________ agent who will show them homes for sale.

Investing your money

bankrupt	profit	risk
bonds	rate	safest
invest	return	stocks

Banks are usually the ______________ place to keep your money, but often not the most profitable. Historically speaking, the interest ______________ given by banks is usually far less than the ______________ on investment that comes from stocks and bonds. However, there is also more ______________ when you ______________ in stocks and bonds than keeping your money in the bank. What is the difference between stocks and bonds? When you purchase ______________, you become a shareholder, which means you are a part owner of a business. And therefore, the more ______________ the company earns, the higher your return on investment will be. When you purchase ______________, you are essentially lending money to a company or government at a fixed rate of return. In the event that the company or government goes ______________, bondholders get paid before shareholders. Therefore, bonds are usually considered to be less risky than stocks.

Collocation match-up: Part 2 *Match the following banking words with their collocations.*

debit	go	invest
default	interest	real

1. ______________ bankrupt
2. ______________ on a loan
3. ______________ rate
4. ______________ estate
5. ______________ card
6. ______________ in stocks

Crossword: Banking and personal finance

Across

2. Paper money.
6. How profitable your investment is: ______ on investment.
7. Bills or coin.
8. Take money out of the bank.
10. A person who works at a bank.
11. A card that lets you withdraw money from your bank: ______ card.
14. Money that you borrow.
20. Money that your bank charges you for withdrawing funds or using ATMs: a transaction ______.
21. Another word for money.
22. A person who buys stocks or bonds.
26. An exchange of money or goods.
29. Another word for property: real ______.
30. Money that you owe someone.
31. A financial policy that pays you compensation in the event of loss, damage, or death.

Down

1. Put money in the bank.
2. Fail at a business: Go ______.
3. Investments that make you part owner of a company.
4. A monthly written record of your bank account.
5. A plan for spending money.
9. Invest in many different things so that you will not lose everything if one particular business fails.
12. Money spent purchasing something in hopes of selling it for profit in the future.
13. Money you give to your bank every month when you have a mortgage: a mortgage ______.
15. A card that lets you borrow money to make purchases: ______ card.
16. The cost of borrowing money.
17. Not be able to pay money that you owe: ______ on a loan.
18. The chance that an investment will lose money.
19. A loan used to buy a house.
23. Money you receive when you retire.
24. How much money you have in your account.
25. Anything of value that you own.
27. Metal money.
28. Investments where you lend money to a company in return for a fixed rate of interest.

PUZZLE

12·6

Word search: Banking and personal finance *Find the following words in the grid.*

```
Q P C W H D E B I T C A R D Z D B S Z H V W N I
C I F I S M L A C E T T P U K O U P S V F F T G
O X K M D B O N D A B E B W M R D E H V R N S A
L N B U B M A K F E S N L J W R G C Q L E V B B
L J A W A O N J D F Q H F L A S E U T M C H W C
A L L J I R Q J V N U W M C E T T L Y B V F G S
T I A R E T I R E M E N T E Y R S A O G C Z R J
E N N B P G H N P I Z I D F I A P T T K Q Q H J
R S C C E A L D V W D A L S N N E E O E S P G D
A U E E H G S U R E D I V E R S I F Y C M V W N
L R Y S C E Y N R A S A Z I S A I W W E K E O E
L A Q V E L R C Y Z W T H A N C G S A B Z I N T
P N R F G U A R A N T E E D H T N K K I S M L T
I C X I T D E P O S I T E R M I E A C N V Y F U
A E Q E S K C S A V I N G S O O H R E Z G V T R
N T R M N K E X P E N S E C U N S P E R F D H D
V F C G Z A C R E D I T C H E C K C D S M Y A Z
O K J C H E C K I N G D H D Z Y W Z N L T N J A
```

asset
balance
bank
bond
budget
cash
checking
coins
collateral
credit card
credit check
debit card
debt

deposit
diversify
expense
fees
funds
guaranteed
insurance
interest
invest
loan
mortgage
payee
payment

pension
retirement
return
risk
savings
speculate
statement
stock
teller
term
transaction
withdraw

Idiom puzzle: Money idioms *Complete the money-related idioms below. Use the symbols below the blanks to help you solve the idioms.*

1. Expensive:	COST A PRETTY _ _ _ _ _ Δ 20 ★ ★
2. Done very cheaply:	ON A SHOESTRING _ _ _ _ _ _ ♦ Ω ♥ ▲ ◐ 8
3. Have no money at all:	FLAT _ _ _ _ _ ♦ ▼ 2 ◐
4. Pay for everyone:	FOOT THE _ _ _ _ ♦ ■ 19 ◈
5. Have extra cash to spend:	MONEY TO _ _ _ _ ♦ Ω ▼ 3
6. Try hard not to spend:	SCRIMP AND _ _ _ _ 7 ♣ 21 ◐
7. Very common:	A _ _ _ _ A DOZEN ♥ ■ 1 ◐
8. Have a great change in fortune:	GO FROM RAGS TO _ _ _ _ _ _ ▼ ■ ● 4 ♠
9. Have something valuable but not know it:	SITTING ON A _ _ _ _ _ _ _ _ ▲ 15 23 ♥ Σ ■ ★ ◐
10. Put money away for an emergency:	SAVE FOR A _ _ _ _ _ DAY ▼ ♣ 6 ★
11. Barely earn enough money to pay your bills:	MAKE ENDS _ _ _ _ Σ ◐ ◐ 14
12. Very inexpensive:	DIRT _ _ _ _ _ ● 9 ◐ ♣ Δ
13. Save:	_ _ _ _ _ _ _ _ AWAY ♠ Ω 22 ▼ ▼ ◐ ◈
14. Make some very bad investments:	LOSE YOUR _ _ _ _ _ ♠ ■ 11 ▣
15. Have the ability to make money easily:	HAVE THE MIDAS _ _ _ _ _ ▣ 13 Ω ●
16. Charging way too high a price:	HIGHWAY _ _ _ _ _ _ _ ▼ 12 ♦ ♦ ◐ ▼ 5
17. A small amount of money:	CHICKEN _ _ _ _ 16 ◐ ◐ ♥
18. Be careful when purchasing something:	LET THE BUYER _ _ _ _ _ _ ♦ 10 17 ▼ ◐
19. Cut back on spending money:	TIGHTEN YOUR _ _ _ _ ♦ ◐ 18 ▣

PUZZLE

12·8

Code breaker *Use the number code in Puzzle 12•7 to solve the proverb about money.*

Money causes many problems.

__ __ __ __ __   __ __   __ __ __   __ __ __ __   __ __   __ __ __   __ __ __ __.

1 2 3 4 5   6 7   8 9 10   11 12 13 14   15 16   17 18 19   20 21 22 23

The economy

·13·

VOCABULARY

asset
bailout
capital
central bank
commodity
consumer
corporation
currency
demand
economic indicators
exchange rate
export
free enterprise
GDP (gross domestic product)
goods
human resources
import
inflation
monopoly
natural resources
producer
raw materials
regulate
scarcity
service
speculate
stimulus
supply
surplus
tariff
trade
unemployment

PUZZLE 13·1

Definition match-up: The economy *Match the following definitions with words from the vocabulary list.*

1. Another word for company: ____________________
2. A country's money: ____________________
3. Extra of something: ____________________
4. Not enough of something: ____________________
5. The main bank of a country: ____________________
6. Control something through laws: ____________________
7. Something of economic value: ____________________
8. A market with only one seller: ____________________
9. A system in which private business can operate freely: ____________________
10. Money needed to start a business: ____________________
11. A person who buys goods or services: ____________________
12. A person who makes goods or services: ____________________
13. Government aid to a failing business: ____________________
14. How much of something exists: ____________________

15. How much of something is wanted: ____________________

16. How much foreign currency costs: ____________________

17. How much is produced in a country: ____________________

18. Things that tell us about the economy (like the inflation rate): ____________________

PUZZLE 13·2

Labeling: Economic terms *Attach the following economy-related labels to the lists of words.*

Economic downturns	Human resources	Market forces
Goods	International trade	Services

1. recession, depression, economic meltdown ____________________
2. supply, demand ____________________
3. transporting goods, teaching a class ____________________
4. televisions, bread ____________________
5. employees, labor, skilled workers ____________________
6. imports, exports ____________________

PUZZLE 13·3

Matching: Economic collocations *Match the following words with their collocations below.*

balance	free	per	supply
central	goods	raw	tariff
division	human	real	trade
exchange	market	stock	

1. ____________ bank
2. ____________ estate
3. ____________ capita
4. ____________ and services
5. ____________ materials
6. ____________ enterprise
7. ____________ and demand
8. ____________ resources
9. ____________ on imports
10. ____________ of trade

11. ______________ of labor

12. ______________ forces

13. ______________ rate

14. ______________ market

15. ______________ war

PUZZLE **13·4**

Fill in the blanks: The economy *Complete the following paragraphs by filling in the blanks using the words provided.*

Goods and services

cut	owner	touch
goods	service	transported
intangible	tangible	
market	teach	

A ______________ is a place where goods and services are bought and sold. ______________ are things that people buy and sell such as TVs, computers, cars, food, and books. They are physical things that you can actually hold or ______________. If something can be held or touched we say that it is ______________. Goods can be ______________ from one place to another. When you pay for a good, you become the ______________ of that good.

A ______________, on the other hand, is something that you pay other people to do for you. For example, having someone ______________ your hair or ______________ you a class are examples of services. Services are said to be ______________.

Consumers and producers

bakery	factories	purchase
capital	human	raw
consumers	producers	

People who use goods and services are called ______________. When you ______________ a loaf of bread and eat it, you are a consumer. ______________, on the other hand, are people who make goods and services to be consumed. If you work in a ______________ and make a loaf of bread, then you are a producer. Many goods are produced in ______________.

In order to produce goods or services, producers need three things as inputs. First they need ______________ goods, which include the tools, buildings, and machinery they use to make things. Producers also need ______________ materials to make their finished products. Finally, they need ______________ resources to control the machinery and manage everything.

Market forces

demand	monopoly	supply
drop	rise	surplus
forces	scarcity	

Supply and demand are market ______________ that determine the price of goods and services. ______________ is how much of a good or service is produced. ______________ is how much of a good or service is wanted. If there is more supply than there is demand, we say there is a ______________ of that good or service. In this case, the price of the good or service usually starts to ______________. If demand for a good or service outstrips supply, we say there is a ______________ of that good or service. In this case, the price usually starts to ______________. When there is only one seller in a market, that seller has a ______________ and can charge whatever price the seller wishes.

International trade

balance	free	tariffs
exchange	import	trade
export	impose	

International trade is the ______________ of goods and services between countries. When a good is bought from another country it is called an ______________. When a good is sold to another country it is called an ______________. The difference between the amount and value of imports and the value of exports is called the ______________ of trade. Sometimes, governments ______________ taxes on imports to protect their local industries. These taxes are called ______________. If the other country feels these tariffs are unfair, it may impose tariffs as well, and then a ______________ war begins. A ______________ trade agreement is when two countries agree to remove all tariffs between the countries.

Word search: The economy *Find the following words in the grid.*

```
D U V C W G P R O F I T P S H A R E S H J R W B
Y E X C H A N G E R A T E D S B D O U V Q G S L
C O M P E T I T I O N C P U V A S U P P L Y X W
E E R A W M A T E R I A L S R E G U L A T E R U
C X N S N H Q I V V K U T T A R I F F L P P F P
C U P T I D V G R J M S P E C U L A T I O N C I
C Y R O R K J E E I O A U E S C A R C I T Y U G
R B I R R E S S T C I C O N S U M E R A B C U V
E I A B E T P S Z H U M A N R E S O U R C E S U
D C N N A N P R O D U C E R I N D I C A T O R S
I H O T K I C A E M P L O Y E E I N D U S T R Y
T A V N E R L Y U N E M P L O Y M E N T P F L G
L F A F O R U O F R E E E N T E R P R I S E B Y
U X D X T M E P U G O U T S O U R C E J K Z Q N
L U T Y B J Y S T T O V R I N V E S T M E N T R
A O W M L G P V T C C O R P O R A T I O N B E T
G V S U R P L U S N Y F D I N F L A T I O N T J
W I R S B Z F V R E C E S S I O N I M P O R T Q
```

bailout
bankruptcy
competition
consumer
corporation
costs
credit
currency
demand
economy
employee
entrepreneur
exchange rate
export

free enterprise
goods
human resources
import
indicators
industry
inflation
interest
investment
loss
outsource
producer
profit
raw materials

recession
regulate
scarcity
services
shares
speculation
stimulus
supply
surplus
tariff
trade
unemployment

PUZZLE 13·6

Crossword: The economy

Across

4. Get people from outside the company (or even outside the country) to do work for your company.
5. Anything of economic value that a company has.
7. A good that is sold to the consumer: ______ product.
9. How much money you earn.
10. Basic materials from which something is manufactured: ______ materials.

Down

1. The opposite of profit.
2. The difference in value of imports and exports: the ______ of trade.
3. A time when the government helps a failing business (usually through loans).
6. A tax that is levied on imports.
7. Supply and demand: market ______.
8. Sell goods to another country.
12. How much of a good people want to buy.

Across

11. Buy goods from another country.
12. How much money you owe.
14. Not enough goods and services to satisfy demand.
16. Money you borrow from someone.
17. A place where goods and services are sold.
19. The amount that prices rise over time.
20. Trade without any tariffs: ______ trade.
23. How much of a good is available to sell.
24. A time when the economy is bad.
25. A time when workers refuse to work.
27. The people who work in a business: ______ resources.
28. The number of people not working: the ______ rate.
29. A system in which private business can operate freely: free ______.
31. A group of workers who get together to protect their rights.
32. A country's money.

Down

13. The money used to start up a business.
15. Extra money you pay when you borrow money.
18. Money you earn above what you spend in a business.
21. How much of one country's money you get for another country's money: the ______ rate.
22. A person who buys goods or services.
23. An excess of goods and services.
26. A situation where there is only one seller.
30. Money that the government collects from citizens.

PUZZLE 13·7

Word paths: Economics *Find and circle the secret words below by following a connected path through the maze. Some words may overlap.*

S	E	R	V	I	E	X	P	O	R	T
I		A		C		B		O		S
M	A	R	K	E	T	E	C	E	M	U
P		O		M		S		R		S
O	Y	L	P	P	U	S	I	C	O	N
R		N		G		I		U		O
T	D	E	M	A	E	O	C	R	O	I
S		N		N		N		R		T
R	A	D	G	D	P	C	N	E	O	A
T		E		M		Y		Y		L
I	N	T	E	R	E	S	T	I	N	F

1. The increase in the price level. _ _ _ _ _ _ _ _ _
2. A person who uses goods and services. _ _ _ _ _ _ _ _
3. A time when the economy is bad. _ _ _ _ _ _ _ _ _
4. Work you pay people to do for you. _ _ _ _ _ _ _
5. Goods sold to another country. _ _ _ _ _ _ _
6. Goods bought from another country. _ _ _ _ _ _ _
7. The cost of borrowing money. _ _ _ _ _ _ _ _
8. How much of a good is available. _ _ _ _ _ _
9. How much of a good is wanted. _ _ _ _ _ _
10. A country's money. _ _ _ _ _ _ _ _
11. Where goods are bought and sold. _ _ _ _ _ _
12. Short for gross domestic product. _ _ _
13. The exchange of goods between countries. _ _ _ _ _

Hidden message: Economic idiom *Use the remaining letters to uncover an idiom related to economics.*

A good time to do business:

_   _ _ _ _ _ _ _ _ _   _ _ _ _ _ _ _ _ _ _

PUZZLE
13·8

Idiom puzzle: Money-related idioms *Complete the money-related idioms below. Use the symbols below the blanks to help you solve the idioms.*

1. Not make money, but not lose money: B R E A K _ _ _ _
   ♥ 6 25
2. Sold out: O U T O F _ _ _ _ _
   ▼ 27 8 41 ●
3. Save money: C U T _ _ _ _ _ _ _
   ◐ 2 ▲ 30 ♥ ▲ 38
4. An estimate: A B A L L P A R K _ _ _ _ _ _
   7 ♣ ■ Δ 22 42
5. More value for your money: M O R E _ _ _ _ F O R Y O U R B U C K
   5 ♠ 34 ■
6. Losing money: I N T H E _ _ _
   9 ♥ ◈
7. Making a profit: I N T H E _ _ _ _ _
   ♦ 14 ♠ ◐ 33
8. Not enough of something: I N S H O R T _ _ _ _ _ _
   ▼ Δ 19 17 ★ 28
9. Increase morale in the company: _ _ _ _ _ T H E T R O O P S
   ▲ ♠ ★ 31 32
10. Put a new product on the market: _ _ _ _ _ _ _ A P R O D U C T
    ▲ 39 ★ ★ 21 24 Σ
11. Become bankrupt: G O _ _ _ _ _ U P
    ♦ ♥ 1 ★ 11
12. Start a business: S E T U P _ _ _ _
    ▼ ▣ 12 20
13. A chance you are willing to take: A C A L C U L A T E D _ _ _ _
    ▲ 26 ▼ 4
14. A type of advertising: W O R D O F _ _ _ _ _
    Ω 29 13 Σ ▣
15. Do what is expected or promised: D E L I V E R T H E _ _ _ _ _
    ■ 3 35 ◈ ▼
16. Sell well: S E L L L I K E _ _ _ _ _ _ _ _ _
    ▣ 23 36 ♠ ● 15 ▼
17. A place to negotiate: T H E _ _ _ _ _ _ _ _ _ _ T A B L E
    ♦ ♠ ▲ ■ ♠ ♣ 40 ♣ ■
18. Being planned: I N T H E _ _ _ _ _
    18 ▲ ● ▼
19. Be the dominant seller: C O R N E R T H E _ _ _ _ _ _
    Ω 16 ▲ 37 10 Σ

Code breaker: Contrasting proverbs *Use the number code in Puzzle 13•8 to solve the two contrasting proverbs.*

Proverb 1

Be cautious.

__ __ __ __   __ __ __ __ __ __   __ __ __   __ __ __ __.

1 2 3 4   5 6 7 8 9 10   11 12 13   14 15 16 17

Proverb 2

Act quickly before you lose your chance.

__ __ __ __ __ __ __ __ __ __ __   __ __ __ __   __ __ __ __ __ __   __ __ __ __.

18 19 20 21 22 23 24 25 26 27 28   29 30 31 32   33 34 35 36 37 38   39 40 41 42

Life science

·14·

VOCABULARY

adaptation	herbivore	predator
carnivore	heredity	prey
cell	hominid	primate
chromosome	instinct	reproduction
classification	invertebrate	reptile
ecosystem	mammal	scavenger
evolution	mutation	species
fauna	offspring	symbiosis
flora	omnivore	trait
gene	organism	vertebrate
habitat	parasite	

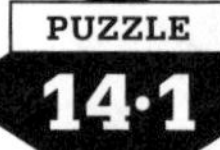

PUZZLE 14·1

Definition match-up: Life science *Match the following definitions with words from the vocabulary list. More than one word may fit some of the definitions.*

1. The plants that live in a region: ________________________
2. The animals that live in a region: ________________________
3. An animal that eats plants: ________________________
4. An animal that eats other animals: ________________________
5. A characteristic of an animal: ________________________
6. The passing of traits from adults to offspring: ________________________
7. A living thing: ________________________
8. An animal that hunts other animals: ________________________
9. An animal that is hunted by other animals: ________________________
10. An animal with a backbone: ________________________
11. Sorting of animals into groups based on common traits: ________________________

12. The place where an animal lives: ________________________

13. The smallest unit of life: ________________________

14. A trait or behavior that helps an animal survive: ________________________

PUZZLE

14·2

Collocation match-up: Life science *Match the following words with their collocations.*

food	natural	recessive	survival
life	predator	sexual	symbiotic

1. _____________ gene
2. _____________ web
3. _____________ reproduction
4. _____________ of the fittest
5. _____________ cycle
6. _____________ relationship
7. _____________ and prey
8. _____________ selection

PUZZLE

14·3

Ranking: Life science *The following words represent groups of animals. Rank the groups from largest (1) to smallest (5).*

____ primates ____ vertebrates ____ hominids ____ mammals ____ humans

PUZZLE 14·4

Labeling: Life science *Attach the following labels to the lists of words below.*

Behavioral adaptations	Relations in a food web
Heredity	Relationships between organisms
Insect life cycle	Theory of evolution
Physical/structural adaptations	Vertebrates
Plant reproduction	

1. camouflage, stinging cells, sharp claws and teeth ____________
2. decomposer, predator, prey ____________
3. amphibians, reptiles, mammals ____________
4. cone, pollen, seed ____________
5. hibernation, migration, playing dead ____________
6. larva, metamorphosis, pupa ____________
7. mutation, natural selection, survival of the fittest ____________
8. chromosome, genes, dominant/recessive trait ____________
9. parasitic, mutualism, symbiotic ____________

PUZZLE 14·5

Word sort: Types of animals *Sort the following animals into their categories.*

clam	gorilla	lobster	shrimp	toad
crab	horse	octopus	snail	turtle
frog	lizard	salamander	snake	whale

REPTILE	MAMMAL	MOLLUSK	CRUSTACEAN	AMPHIBIAN
________	________	________	________	________
________	________	________	________	________
________	________	________	________	________

Fill in the blanks: Life science *Complete the following paragraphs by filling in the blanks using the words provided.*

Characteristics of living organisms

cells	energy	grow	reproduce
characteristics	environment	organisms	stimuli

All living ______________ share a few basic ______________. For example, all living things are composed of ______________. As well, all living things get ______________ from food. Living things ______________ larger during their life cycle. They also respond to ______________ in their ______________. Finally, a species would die out without offspring, so living things also need to ______________.

Animal classification

biologists	crustaceans	invertebrates	reptiles	traits
classified	hand	mammals	sort	

People who study living organisms are called ______________. Biologists ______________ animals into groups with common ______________. For example, animals can be ______________ into vertebrates and ______________. Vertebrates can be further classified into fish, birds, ______________, amphibians, and ______________. Invertebrates, on the other ______________, do not have backbones. They can be further divided into smaller groups such as ______________, mollusks, and insects.

The theory of evolution

adaptation	environment	published	selection
claimed	generation	reproduce	survival

When Charles Darwin ______________ his theory of natural ______________ in 1859, he revolutionized the way we look at life on earth. In his theory, Darwin ______________ that organisms better adapted to their ______________ are more likely to survive and ______________. Hence that ______________ is more likely to be passed on to the next ______________ of animals and will eventually spread throughout the population of animals. This theory is also sometimes called the ______________ of the fittest.

The principles of heredity

both	heredity	offspring	recessive
genes	inherited	pass	trait

In biology, a ______________ is a particular way that an organism looks or behaves. ______________ acquire their traits from their parents. The principle that parents ______________ down traits to their offspring is called ______________. The traits an organism exhibits are determined by its ______________. Genes are sections of DNA on chromosomes that are ______________ from the parents. Some genes are ______________, which means that trait will only show up if the offspring receives that gene from ______________ parents.

Relations in a food web

apex	eaten	population	vegetation
balance	grazing	predator	web

A food ______________ is all of the relationships that connect predators and prey in an ecosystem. Some animals can be both ______________ and prey. For example, salmon eat shrimp and smaller fish but are ______________ by seals, whales, and bears. A predator that has no predators is called an ______________ predator. Apex predators are important for maintaining the ______________ of nature. Without apex predators, the ______________ of many species of ______________ animals would increase dramatically. As a result, they would overgraze and destroy ground ______________.

PUZZLE
14·7

Idiom puzzle: Animal idioms *Complete the following animal idioms. Use the symbols below the blanks to help you solve the idioms. Each symbol represents one letter.*

1. A deceptive person:	A _ _ _ _ _ IN THE GRASS ♥ ♦ 4 Ω 28
2. A source of unpredictable trouble:	A CAN OF _ _ _ _ _ ▲ 10 ♠ 25 ♥
3. Save a little money:	_ _ _ _ _ _ _ _ AWAY SOME CASH ♥ Δ ■ 30 ♠ 3 ♣
4. Dying or quitting rapidly:	DROPPING LIKE _ _ _ _ _ 15 ♣ ■ 31 ♥
5. The greatest portion:	THE LION'S _ _ _ _ _ ♥ 2 ★ ♠ 32
6. Very slow:	A SNAIL'S _ _ _ _ 5 20 ◐ ▣
7. Cause problems:	STIR UP A _ _ _ _ _ _ _'_ NEST 27 ▼ ♠ ♦ ▣ 29 ♥
8. Can't see at all:	BLIND AS A _ _ _ ♪ 16 1
9. Be nervous or agitated:	HAVE ANTS IN YOUR _ _ _ _ _ 6 ★ ♦ 14 ♥
10. Mischief, misbehavior, or trickery:	_ _ _ _ _ _ BUSINESS ∞ ▼ 13 Ω 8 ●
11. Don't stir up trouble:	LET SLEEPING _ _ _ _ LIE 9 ▼ 12
12. A relatively unimportant person:	A SMALL _ _ _ 22 ♠ ●
13. Suddenly become quiet:	_ _ _ _ UP ◐ 7 ★ ∞
14. The shortest distance between two points:	AS THE _ _ _ _ FLIES ◐ 21 24 ▲
15. A dangerous person pretending to be good:	A _ _ _ _ IN SHEEP'S CLOTHING ▲ ▼ 18 19
16. Dazed:	LIKE A _ _ _ _ IN HEADLIGHTS 11 ▣ 23
17. Be decisive:	TAKE THE _ _ _ _ BY THE HORNS ♪ Δ 17 ♣
18. Be suspicious:	SMELL A _ _ _ ♠ ★ 26

PUZZLE **14·8**

Code breaker: A proverb about heredity *Use the number code in Puzzle 14•7 to solve the proverb.*

Children grow up to be like their parents.

__ __ __   __ __ __ __ __   __ __ __ __ __'__   __ __ __ __   __ __ __   __ __ __ __
1 2 3   4 5 6 7 8   9 10 11 12 13 14   15 16 17 18   19 20 21   22 23 24 25

__ __ __   __ __ __ __.
26 27 28   29 30 31 32

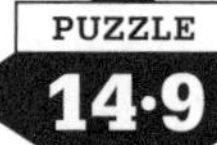

PUZZLE **14·9**

Word paths: Life science *Find and circle the secret words below by following a connected path through the maze. Some words may overlap.*

A	N	O	A	S	M	I	V	O	R	E
I	■	R	■	I	■	N	■	D	■	A
B	O	G	A	N	O	M	F	L	O	R
I	■	G	■	E	■	L	■	A	■	T
H	R	E	P	T	I	L	E	C	T	E
P	■	P	■	T	■	D	■	N	■	T
M	T	R	A	I	O	P	R	I	M	A
A	■	E	■	G	■	W	■	T	■	R
E	H	Y	O	A	T	I	N	S	R	B
R	■	T	■	T	■	O	■	L	■	E
E	D	I	M	U	D	N	V	E	R	T

1. A change in an organism's DNA. __ __ __ __ __ __ __ __
2. A frog or a salamander. __ __ __ __ __ __ __ __ __
3. A behavior that animals are born with. __ __ __ __ __ __ __ __
4. A living thing. __ __ __ __ __ __ __ __
5. Turtle or lizard. __ __ __ __ __ __ __
6. The animal that is hunted. __ __ __ __
7. Something inherited from parents. __ __ __ __ __

8. The passing of traits to offspring. __ __ __ __ __ __ __ __ __ __

9. The basic unit of life. __ __ __ __

10. An animal with a backbone. __ __ __ __ __ __ __ __ __ __

11. The plants in a region. __ __ __ __ __

12. An animal that eats plants and animals. __ __ __ __ __ __ __ __ __

13. A chimp, gorilla, or human. __ __ __ __ __ __ __

Hidden message: A problem idiom *Use the remaining letters to uncover an idiom related to competition.*

Survival of the fittest:

__   __ __ __   __ __ __   __ __ __   __ __ __ __ __

Crossword: Life science *Fill in the correct word to solve the puzzle.*

Across

1. An animal that lives off of another animal.
6. The animals in a region.
8. A behavior or body part that helps an animal survive.
9. The place where an animal is typically found.
11. An animal with a backbone.
12. A relationship between two animals that benefits them both.
15. A basic unit of DNA that controls your traits.
16. A tortoise or a lizard.
18. An animal that eats plants and animals.
21. A living thing.
22. The passing of traits from parents to offspring.

Down

1. An animal that hunts other animals.
2. A particular characteristic of an organism.
3. An animal that eats other animals.
4. The babies of an animal.
5. The relationships between predator and prey in an ecosystem.
7. The plants in a region.
9. An animal that eats plants.
10. A behavior that an animal is born with.
12. The kind of animal.
13. The basic unit of life.
14. A change in an animal's genetic code.
17. Animal like a human or an orangutan.
19. An animal that has live birth and produces milk for its young.
20. An animal that is hunted.

PUZZLE **14·11**

Word scramble: Life science *Use the clues on the left to unscramble the letters and form words used to discuss problems and solutions.*

1. An animal that hunts: D A P R E R O T _ _ _ _ _ _ _ _ (10)
2. An animal that eats plants: E R O V H R E B I _ _ _ _ _ _ _ _ _ (20, 5)
3. An animal with a backbone: T E R V E T A R B E _ _ _ _ _ _ _ _ _ _ (14)
4. An organism that lives off of another: S I T E R A A P _ _ _ _ _ _ _ _ (21, 12)
5. An inherited characteristic: I R A T T _ _ _ _ _ (7)
6. A place where an animal lives: T A B T H A I _ _ _ _ _ _ _ (2, 4)
7. A plant or an animal: G A N O R M S I _ _ _ _ _ _ _ _ (17, 9)
8. A snake, turtle, or lizard: T R E L I P E _ _ _ _ _ _ _ (3)
9. A human or gorilla: M A R I P E T _ _ _ _ _ _ _ (6)
10. One type of organism: C I E S P S E _ _ _ _ _ _ _ (19)
11. An animal's babies: G N F F S R P I O _ _ _ _ _ _ _ _ _ (11, 15)
12. A section of DNA on a chromosome: G N E E _ _ _ _ (23)
13. A theory explaining how animals change: L U T O V E N I O _ _ _ _ _ _ _ _ _ (8, 22)
14. A change in an animal's genetic code: T U M T I O N A _ _ _ _ _ _ _ _ (1, 16)
15. Passing of genes from parents to offspring: H D E E R Y I T _ _ _ _ _ _ _ _ (13, 18)

PUZZLE **14·12**

Code breaker *Use the number code in Puzzle 14•11 to solve the idiom below.*

An unimportant person in a business or other organization:

_ _ _   _ _ _ _ _ _   _ _   _ _ _   _ _ _ _   _ _ _ _ _

1 2 3   4 5 6 7 8 9   10 11   12 13 14   15 16 17 18   19 20 21 22 23

The environment: Issues and conservation

·15·

VOCABULARY

Environmental issues

acid rain
bush meat
carbon dioxide
climate change
contamination
deforestation
desertification
detergent
disposable
endangered species
exhaust fumes
extinct
fossil fuel
global warming
greenhouse effect
habitat loss
invasive species
landfill
oil spill
overfishing
ozone layer
pesticide
polar ice cap
pollution/smog
roadkill
toxic waste
urban sprawl
whaling

Definition match-up: Environmental issues *Match the following definitions with words from the vocabulary list.*

1. The gradual rise in Earth's average temperature: ______________________
2. Altered weather patterns due to global warming: ______________________
3. A species not native to an area (often harmful to native species): ______________________
4. An economic activity that results in the collapse of fish populations: ______________________
5. Something you use once and then throw away: ______________________
6. A place where waste is buried and disposed of: ______________________
7. Animals killed by motorists: ______________________
8. The uncontrolled expansion of cities: ______________________
9. A chemical used to kill weeds or insects: ______________________
10. A chemical used to clean things: ______________________
11. The destruction of forests: ______________________

12. The process of changing a region into a desert: ____________________

13. A greenhouse gas: ____________________

14. Environmentally damaging rain caused by atmospheric pollution: ____________________

15. Waste gases ejected from an engine or a factory: ____________________

16. A species that is nearing extinction: ____________________

17. No longer exists (as in a species): ____________________

18. An ice sheet that covers the North Pole: ____________________

19. The destruction of wildlife homes (usually due to development): ____________________

20. The hunting of large marine mammals for food: ____________________

21. Part of the atmosphere that blocks UV rays: ____________________

22. The trapping of heat in the atmosphere by greenhouse gases like carbon dioxide and methane: ____________________

PUZZLE **15·2**

Collocation match-up: Environmental issues *Match the following words with their collocations.*

acid	endangered	greenhouse	oil
bush	exhaust	habitat	toxic
climate	fossil	invasive	urban
disposable	global	ozone	

1. ____________ fuel
2. ____________ loss
3. ____________ species
4. ____________ species
5. ____________ effect
6. ____________ meat
7. ____________ rain
8. ____________ cup
9. ____________ warming
10. ____________ spill
11. ____________ waste
12. ____________ fumes
13. ____________ change
14. ____________ sprawl
15. ____________ layer

PUZZLE 15·3

Labeling: Environmental issues *Attach the following environment-related labels to the lists of words below.*

Atmospheric gases	Environmental disasters	Fossil fuels
Causes of extinction	Examples of climate change	Sources of air pollution
Endangered species	Extinct species	Threatened habitats

1. habitat loss, poaching ______________
2. oil spill, nuclear meltdown ______________
3. dodo bird, Barbary lion ______________
4. blue whales, African elephants ______________
5. coal, oil ______________
6. carbon dioxide, oxygen ______________
7. desertification, melting polar ice cap ______________
8. rain forests, coral reefs ______________
9. car exhaust, factory emissions ______________

PUZZLE 15·4

Fill in the blanks: Environmental issues *Complete the following paragraphs by filling in the blanks using the words provided.*

Environmental pollution

contaminates	fertilizers	plastic
detergents	fumes	smog
environmental	leaks	toxic

______________ pollution comes from many sources. The exhaust ______________ from motor vehicles produce ______________ that hangs over cities. ______________ used to clean clothes and ______________ used to grow crops contribute to water pollution. ______________ waste dumped into the ground eventually ______________ into the surrounding area and ______________ the soil. ______________ thrown into the oceans can float in the currents for years, killing wildlife that mistakes it for food.

Global warming and climate change

climate	gases	livestock
dioxide	global	sea
fossil	greenhouse	temperature

Scientists believe that human activity can actually change the Earth's ______________. By increasing greenhouse ______________ in the atmosphere, humans may be causing ______________ warming due to the ______________ effect. Greenhouse gases, which include carbon ______________ and methane, trap heat in the atmosphere, causing a rise in the average global ______________. As temperatures rise, the water trapped in ice will be released into the oceans, resulting in a catastrophic rise in ______________ level. Where do these greenhouse gases come from? Carbon dioxide is produced by burning ______________ fuels, and methane is a by-product of raising ______________.

Habitat loss

bush	clear	extinct	loss	nesting
change	deforestation	hunting	lumber	wetlands

The greatest threat to wildlife is not the ______________ of wild animals for ______________ meat as many people might think, but is instead habitat ______________. The causes of habitat loss are varied, but a few causes stand out. One major cause is ______________, especially in the tropical rain forests of the world. As farmers ______________ the land so they can plant crops and loggers cut down trees for ______________, many species of wildlife go ______________ and the Earth's biodiversity decreases. Another major cause of habitat loss is unregulated development of ______________, where many species of birds and insects live. As builders fill in these lands to build new suburbs, important ______________ grounds for endangered birds disappear. Finally, climate ______________ can also destroy habitat, forcing animals to move into areas with a climate suitable to them.

Decreasing biodiversity

balance	insects	predators
ecosystem	invasive	species
habitat	living	web

Biodiversity is the variety of ______________ organisms that exist in an area. Biodiversity is important for ensuring a healthy ______________. The loss of one ______________ can sometimes have devastating effects as its disappearance is felt through the food ______________. Species can reproduce out of control if their primary ______________ disappear or starve if their primary food sources disappear. Without pollinating ______________, most of the world's food crops could not be grown. In short, destroying one species can upset the ______________ of nature. ______________ loss, overhunting, and ______________ species are all major causes of biodiversity loss.

Word search: Environmental issues *Find the following words in the grid.*

```
L Y C G R E E N B E L T E D E T E R G E N T N A
F A O E A Z V F E C O S Y S T E M C E T J Z B C
O M N N I Y F A X U U Y C I P R O T E C T E D H
S P T D N B I O D E G R A D A B L E E W Y Q R V
S O A A F S O P R C P E S T I C I D E L Y C Y H
I A M N O I I O P E O E T O X I C W A S T E L V
L C I G R N L L C A R B O N F O O T P R I N T E
F H N E E V S L M V G L O B A L W A R M I N G T
U I A R S A P U W H A L I N G W I L D L I F E Z
E N T E T S I T U Z N X H A B I T A T L O S S E
L G I D R I L I I A I J X U O Z O N E L A Y E R
E K O F U V L O Y G C C O N S E R V A T I O N F
X E N G R E E N H O U S E E F F E C T F H Z M Z
T I A V C U C A R B O N D I O X I D E A J N A W
I R E D U C E D E S E R T I F I C A T I O N U F
N D I S P O S A B L E L R W K E X H A U S T U D
C U S O L A R E N E R G Y A C I D R A I N P H W
T A G E M C O N S U M P T I O N Q C O M P O S T
```

acid rain
biodegradable
carbon dioxide
carbon footprint
compost
conservation
consumption
contamination
desertification
detergent

disposable
ecosystem
endangered
exhaust
extinct
fossil fuel
global warming
greenbelt
greenhouse effect
habitat loss

invasive
landfill
oil spill
organic
ozone layer
pesticide
poaching
pollution
protected
rain forest

recycle
reduce
reuse
smog
solar energy
toxic waste
whaling
wildlife

PUZZLE 15·6

Crossword: Environmental issues

Across

5. The uncontrolled growth of cities: _______ sprawl.
7. A greenhouse gas: _______ dioxide.
8. Waste gases that come from vehicles: _______ fumes.
9. An environmentally destructive rain caused by air pollution: _______ rain.
10. Contamination of the ocean by oil: an oil _______.
12. The cutting down of forests.

Down

1. The destruction of animal homes: _______ loss.
2. A place where garbage is dumped and buried.
3. A chemical that can help plants grow.
4. The trapping of heat in the atmosphere by gases like carbon dioxide and methane: _______ effect.
6. Anything that degrades or harms the environment.
10. Air pollution that hangs over a city.

Across

13. Belonging to a species that no longer exists.
16. A species near extinction: an ______ species.
20. A material that floats in the ocean and is mistaken for food by animals.
22. Coal, oil, and gas: ______ fuels.
23. Catching too many fish to be sustainable.
24. The hunting of whales.

Down

11. A chemical that kills unwanted weeds and insects.
14. Materials that contaminate the soil when dumped: ______ waste.
15. A species that is not native to an area: ______ species.
17. An animal that has been struck by a motor vehicle.
18. A chemical used to clean clothes that can cause water pollution.
19. A part of the atmosphere that blocks UV radiation from reaching the Earth: ______ layer.
21. The increase of the average temperature of the Earth's surface: ______ warming.

VOCABULARY

Environmental conservation

acid rain
biodegradable
biodiversity
carbon footprint
compost
conservation
consumption
eco-friendly
ecosystem
energy efficient
green
greenbelt
hydroelectric energy
leaky faucet
marine park
nature reserve
organic
poaching
protected species
public transportation
recycle
reduce
renewable resource
reuse
solar energy
sustainable development
wildlife
wind turbines

PUZZLE **15·7**

Definition match-up: Environmental conservation *Match the following definitions with words from the vocabulary list.*

1. How much you use of something: ______________
2. Use less of something: ______________
3. Use an object again (like using a jar to hold pencils): ______________
4. Use a material again (like plastic or glass) to make new products: ______________
5. How much greenhouse gas you generate in your daily life: ______________

6. Natural fertilizer made from waste organic materials such as food leftovers: ____________________
7. Energy from the sun: ____________________
8. Energy from flowing water: ____________________
9. Grown without pesticide or other chemicals: ____________________
10. The illegal hunting of animals: ____________________
11. An animal that is protected by law: ____________________
12. The variety of living organisms found in an area: ____________________
13. Land set aside for forests and animals: ____________________
14. Development that goes over long periods of time without destroying the environment: ____________________
15. A region of parks, farms, and nature reserves that surrounds some urban areas: ____________________
16. Not consuming or wasting much energy: ____________________
17. A kind of plastic that breaks down over time: ____________________
18. Buses, subways, and trains: ____________________
19. Another word for animals: ____________________
20. Using resources wisely to protect and preserve the natural environment: ____________________

PUZZLE
15·8

Labeling: Environmental solutions *Attach the following environmental solutions–related labels to the lists of words below.*

Alternative energy sources	Ways to conserve biodiversity
Eco-friendly product labels	Ways to conserve fossil fuels
Things that waste resources	Ways to reduce litter

1. compost, recycle ____________________
2. biodegradable, energy efficient ____________________
3. solar power, wind turbines ____________________
4. prohibit poaching, protect endangered species ____________________
5. incandescent lightbulbs, leaky faucets ____________________
6. ride a bicycle, take public transportation ____________________

Fill in the blanks: Environmental solutions *Complete the following paragraphs by filling in the blanks using the words provided.*

Reducing waste

cloth	glass	purchasing
disposable	landfills	recycle
environmental	ocean	reduce

The garbage we create in our daily lives has a negative ____________ impact. It ends up floating in the ____________ or buried in ____________. There are many things you can do to ____________ the amount of garbage you generate. For example, you can avoid using ____________ products such as paper coffee cups. You can also avoid ____________ products that have excessive wrapping. As well, you can use ____________ bags to carry your groceries instead of plastic or paper bags. Finally, you can ____________ materials such as plastic, ____________, metal, and paper.

Reducing your carbon footprint

carbon	fuel	measure
consumption	greenhouse	public
emissions	livestock	warming

As the challenge of global ____________ becomes more apparent, many environmentally concerned citizens are looking at ways to reduce their ____________ footprint, which can be defined as the net amount of ____________ gases that you generate in your daily life. In essence, your carbon footprint is a ____________ of your impact on the Earth's climate. One way to reduce your carbon footprint is to cut down on your ____________ of meat. The raising of ____________ such as cattle and sheep generates far more ____________ of greenhouse gas than the growing of crops. Another way to reduce your carbon footprint is to use less fossil ____________ in your day-to-day life. You can do this by riding a bicycle or taking ____________ transportation instead of driving your own car.

Protecting endangered species

ban	endangered	passed
biodiversity	enforced	poachers
black	ivory	threat

An ____________ species is a species of animals with so few members left that it is facing extinction. As governments around the world recognize the importance of ____________, many laws have been ____________ protecting endangered species. In spite of this legal protection, many animals have come under ____________ from ____________. For example, rhinos and elephants are hunted illegally for their horns and tusks. Elephant _____________ is a luxury item in some places that is worth a lot of money. Despite the legal _____________ on ivory sales throughout the world, the high _____________ market prices for ivory ensure that there will be incentive for poachers to continue breaking the law. Laws alone will not help the African elephants; the laws must also be _____________.

Using alternative energy sources

alternative	linked	reliance	resources
fossil	power	renewable	wind

The burning of _____________ fuels is a cause for concern for two reasons: one, they are nonrenewable _____________, and two, burning fossil fuels has been _____________ to global warming. One way to reduce our _____________ on fossils fuels is to develop _____________ energy sources such as _____________ turbines and solar _____________. Both wind and sun are _____________ resources, so developing these forms of energy will ensure we have energy to meet our needs in the future.

PUZZLE 15·10

Crossword: Environmental solutions

Across

2. How much you use of something.
6. Coal, oil, and gas: ______ fuels.
8. Use an object again.
9. Environmental solution: Fix a ______ faucet.
12. Environmental solution: Ride a bike instead of driving a ______.
13. Environmental solution: Wear a sweater instead of turning up the ______.

Down

1. Environmental solution: Use ______ products that won't harm the environment.
3. Energy from the sun: ______ energy.
4. The illegal hunting of animals.
5. Environmental solution: ______ plastic, glass, metal, and paper.
7. Development that can continue over a long period of time without destroying the environment: ______ development.

Across (cont.)

14. Environmental solution: Cut ______ on meat consumption.
16. Environmental solution: Use ______ plastic that won't sit in landfills for thousands of years.
18. The amount of greenhouse gas you generate: your carbon ______.
20. Products you use only once like a paper cup.
21. The variety of living organisms in an area.
22. Use resources wisely so that they are not wasted.

Down (cont.)

10. Environmental solution: Reduce the amount of ______ you use when you do laundry.
11. Use less of something.
12. Environmental solution: ______ organic waste instead of throwing it in the garbage.
15. Energy sources that don't consume fossil fuels: ______ energy sources.
17. Environmental solution: Use energy ______ lightbulbs.
19. Environmental solution: Use ______ transportation instead of driving a car.

Human rights

VOCABULARY

abolition	freedom	persecution
abuses	fundamental	prejudice
atrocities	gender	religion
deny	genocide	segregation
deprive	human rights	self-determination
discrimination	impartial	suffrage
due process	inalienable	thought
equality	justice	torture
ethnicity	liberty	universal
expression	minorities	violation

PUZZLE
16·1

Definition match-up: Human rights *Match the following definitions with words from the vocabulary list.*

1. Basic, primary, or having central importance: ______________________
2. The ability to do what you want or make your own decisions: ______________________
3. Having the same rights and responsibilities: ______________________
4. Belonging to everyone: ______________________
5. Cannot be taken away by anyone including the government: ______________________
6. The requirement that the government respect the legal rights of citizens: ______________________
7. Another word for fair: ______________________
8. Male or female: ______________________
9. The racial or cultural background of a person: ______________________
10. A person's beliefs about and way of worshipping a god or gods: ______________________

11. The ending of something (such as slavery): ____________________

12. Treating someone unfairly due to ethnicity, gender, or religion: ____________________

13. Take away something from someone: ____________________

14. Being divided based on ethnicity, gender, or religion: ____________________

15. A disregard or breaking of someone's rights: ____________________

16. Cruel physical or psychological treatment: ____________________

17. Another way to say opinion: ____________________

18. The systematic destruction of an ethnic group: ____________________

19. Horrible acts such as torture or genocide: ____________________

20. Fundamental rights and protections that all people have: ____________________

PUZZLE **16·2**

Fill in the blanks: Human rights *Complete the following paragraphs by filling in the blanks using the words provided.*

Basic principles of human rights

discriminate	gender	principle	torturing
equality	inalienable	rights	violation

Many political philosophers believe that people have fundamental human ____________, which are basic rights belonging to all people. When a government disregards these rights, we say that is a ____________ of human rights. One of the basic principles of human rights is that of ____________, which means that governments should not ____________ against citizens based on ethnicity, ____________, or religion. Segregation based on ethnicity is an example of a violation of this ____________. Another principle of human rights is that they are ____________, which means that governments cannot take them away. ____________ citizens to obtain information during a national emergency is an example of a violation of this principle.

Universal suffrage and the suffragettes

demand	population	universal
deprived	property	vote
discrimination	suffragettes	women

Suffrage means the right to ____________. Most modern democracies have ____________ suffrage, which means that every adult citizen has the right to vote. However, it wasn't like that in the beginning. The first democracies ____________ most of their citizens of that right, including ______________. In these democracies, the vote was usually limited to male citizens who owned ______________. This meant that over half the adult ______________ couldn't vote. Many women who felt this ______________ was unfair formed societies to ______________ the right to vote. These women were called ______________.

Universal declaration of human rights

atrocities	fundamental	minorities	rights
Declaration	genocide	race	slave

After the ______________ committed during World War II, governments around the world felt that human ______________ were not sufficiently protected. During the war, countless millions were forced into work camps and used as ______________ labor. What's worse, the Nazi party embarked on a campaign of ______________, systematically murdering 6 million Jews and other ______________. When the United Nations formed in 1945, as part of its charter, the member nations declared a universal respect for human rights and ______________ freedoms for all "without distinction as to ______________, sex, language, or religion." However, the United Nations Charter didn't sufficiently define what those human rights were. And so, a second document was created to define exactly what those rights were. It is called the Universal ______________ of Human Rights.

Crimes against humanity

abuses	destruction	humanity	torture
classified	genocide	isolated	

The most serious human rights ______________ are called crimes against ______________. In order to be ______________ as a crime against humanity, the atrocities have to be widespread and systematic. Therefore, an ______________ instance of a human rights violation would not be a crime against humanity. Crimes against humanity include ______________, which is the systematic ______________ of an ethnic or religious group. As well as genocide, other violations of human rights that are classified as crimes against humanity include ______________, enslavement, and even forced deportations if they are committed on a large scale.

Crossword: Human rights

Across

1. The systematic destruction of an ethnic or religious group.
3. Not let somebody have something (such as their rights).
6. The owning of people as if they were property (usually for the purpose of forcing them to work).
10. Belonging to everyone.
11. A fair trial: due ______.
12. The right to say what you think: free ______.

Down

1. Male or female.
2. Can't be taken away by government under any circumstances.
4. Another way to say, "without bias or prejudice."
5. The beliefs that a person holds about a god or gods.
6. The right to vote.
7. Another word for freedom.
8. Basic or primary.

Across

16. The right to do what you want.
19. Cruel physical or psychological treatment.
20. Treating someone unfairly based on gender, religion, or ethnicity.
21. The racial or cultural background of a person.

Down

9. The act of punishing or harming someone based on his or her ethnic or religious background.
13. An unfavorable view based solely on ethnic or religious group.
14. Fundamental rights that all people have.
15. Having the same rights and responsibilities.
17. The ending of a practice (such as slavery).
18. Torture is a ______ of human rights.

PUZZLE **16·4**

Word search: Human rights *Find the following words in the grid.*

```
S E L F D E T E R M I N A T I O N M R N S F B M
W Y W U Z W A H W J U S T I C E Q U A L I T Y P
J D S Y Z O L X T S P H H U N I V E R S A L A N
W W E J G U X I Y W W G X O S R V G T N N L O E
J V A T R O C I T I E S A E M L F W O J N I D D
D C U C H C G E N D E R S N K H I I J A S I R T
S E G R E G A T I O N U O V R Z T B E S C B E Q
D V I O L A T I O N B I V C P A W R E O B F C L
T U M M P Z R E H A T N Q C N U U R N R W G J L
H A E Y P V G S G U W A G I X T P E K V T E O N
O O D P B A M L C M T L M M R X G E P S R Y H G
U R S E R O R E Q Y W I X O E A B O L I T I O N
G F X F D O S T N Y R E T H N I C I T Y S B G B
H J F E B R C E I C U N N Y D E P R I V E W O K
T U E I E P D E S A W A M I N O R I T I E S U V
S R L P N C O I S V L B P R E J U D I C E J R C
F I I S Y L D K K S D L K H U M A N R I G H T S
F U N D A M E N T A L E R E L I G I O N B Y D O
```

abolition	deny	due process	expression
abuses	deprive	equality	freedom
atrocities	discrimination	ethnicity	fundamental

gender	justice	religion	torture
genocide	liberty	segregation	universal
human rights	minorities	self-determination	violation
impartial	persecution	suffrage	
inalienable	prejudice	thought	

International relations

·17·

VOCABULARY

alliance	domestic policy	national interest
ambassador	embargo	negotiations
arms control	embassy	NGO
arms race	foreign policy	reciprocity
border	globalization	regional bloc
capital	government	sanctions
collective security	hegemon	sovereignty
cooperation	humanitarian	trade
deterrence	imperialism	treaty
diplomat	multinational	United Nations
disarmament	nation-state	

PUZZLE
17·1

Definition match-up: International relations *Match the following definitions with words from the vocabulary list.*

1. Any written agreement between nations: ____________________
2. An agreement of military friendship: ____________________
3. Working together to accomplish shared goals: ____________________
4. The political center of a country: ____________________
5. The group of people that rule a country: ____________________
6. Short for nongovernmental organization: ____________________
7. Another word for country: ____________________
8. Any official representing his or her country abroad: ____________________
9. The chief diplomatic officer a country sends to any other country: ____________________
10. The building or compound where a diplomatic mission has its offices (but also refers to the diplomatic mission itself): ____________________
11. A corporation that has operations in more than one country: ____________________

12. What is good for a country: ______________________
13. Talks that are held between two parties in the hopes of reaching an agreement: ______________________
14. A competition between nations to have the strongest military: ______________________
15. Penalties (such as a trade embargo) given to a country for violating international law: ______________________
16. Measures taken to prevent or discourage a hostile action by another state: ______________________
17. The principle that the same benefits given to another state should be received from that state as well: ______________________
18. The authority of a nation to govern itself: ______________________
19. A line that separates two countries: ______________________
20. The domination of one country by another: ______________________

PUZZLE
17·2

Collocation match-up: International relations *Match the following words with their collocations.*

arms	cultural	multinational	regional
arms	diplomatic	nation	trade
balance	humanitarian	nongovernmental	the United

1. ______________ organization
2. ______________ imperialism
3. ______________ aid
4. ______________ race
5. ______________ mission
6. ______________ control
7. ______________ embargo
8. ______________-state
9. ______________ bloc
10. ______________ of power
11. ______________ Nations
12. ______________ corporations

PUZZLE 17·3

Fill in the blanks: International relations *Complete the following paragraphs by filling in the blanks using the words provided.*

Diplomatic relations

ambassador	diplomat	mission
benefit	embassy	negotiations
conflict	interests	resolution

______________ are talks between official representatives of two countries. Two reasons that countries negotiate are ______________ and cooperation. Whenever national interests come into conflict, negotiations are needed to find a peaceful ______________. Whenever nations have mutual ______________, negotiations are needed to make sure both countries ______________. A group of official representatives that travel to another country for negotiations is called a diplomatic ______________. The head of the mission is called the ______________, and anybody who is a member of that mission is called a ______________. The building and compound where the ambassador works is often called the ______________ (though technically speaking the term refers to the diplomatic mission itself).

International cooperation

barriers	greenhouse	receives	resources
cooperate	mutual	reciprocity	whaling

There are many ways that countries ______________ to promote their ______________ interests. For example, countries often benefit economically from reducing ______________ to trade such as tariffs and quotas. Countries also cooperate to protect the environment and manage the Earth's shared ______________ such as the ocean and the atmosphere. Agreements on ______________ and reducing ______________ gases are examples of this kind of cooperation. One principle of international cooperation is the principle of ______________, whereby one nation extends the same rights and benefits to another nation that it ______________ from that nation.

International organizations

Borders	multinational	organization	sovereign
independent	nonprofit	profits	United

An international ______________ is an organization with international membership or with an international presence. There are many types of international organizations. Some organizations such as Doctors Without ______________ and the International Red Cross are ______________ NGOs. NGO is short for nongovernmental organization, which means that an NGO is ______________ of government control. Another type of international organization is a ______________ corporation. These are large companies that have operations in more than one country. Unlike NGOs, the purpose of multinational corporations is to generate ______________ for their shareholders. Finally, some international organizations have ______________ states as members. The ______________ Nations is an example of this kind of organization.

Balance of power

alliances	collective	deter	hegemon
balance	combine	dominate	World

The ______________ of power is a theory that nations will organize themselves so that no single state can ______________ the others. As one nation or group of nations becomes powerful, other nations will ______________ their power and influence to counter this rising power. This cooperation between countries to counter a threat is sometimes called ______________ security. In theory, collective security is meant to prevent a ______________ from dominating other countries. The member countries often sign military ______________ with the hope that it will ______________ aggression. Though this does work at times, it can also result in expanded conflict when alliance blocs come into conflict, such as happened in ______________ War I.

PUZZLE 17·4

Crossword: International relations

Across

4. The compound and building where an ambassador works.
5. Discourage or prevent an attack.
10. Punishments imposed on a country for violations of international law.
11. A military agreement of friendship.
12. The line that divides two countries.
14. The authority of a nation to govern itself.
17. Work together.

Down

1. Good for a country: in the national ______.
2. Policy that deals with international issues: ______ policy.
3. The combination of weaker nations to deter aggression: ______ security.
4. The prohibition of trade with a country.
5. The practice of conducting negotiations between states.
6. The chief diplomat sent to another country.

Across (cont.)

19. The principle of extending benefits to another country and receiving the same benefits from that country.
20. A major international organization: the _______ Nations.
21. A competition to build the strongest military: _______ race.
22. A company that operates in many countries: _______ corporation.
23. Policy that deals with internal issues: _______ policy.
24. Any written agreement between two countries.

Down (cont.)

7. The political center of a country.
8. Any official representative of a country that deals with representatives of other countries.
9. The distribution of military power so that no single state can dominate: _______ of power.
13. Talks that have the aim of reaching an agreement.
15. The domination of one country by another.
16. The group of people who rule a country.
18. Something countries can cooperate over: _______ interests.

Word search: International relations *Find the following words in the grid.*

A	C	O	L	L	E	C	T	I	V	E	S	E	C	U	R	I	T	Y	O	Z	T	X	C
R	F	P	P	M	G	X	Q	U	O	J	A	M	B	A	S	S	A	D	O	R	J	B	S
M	H	M	U	L	T	I	N	A	T	I	O	N	A	L	N	W	W	Z	E	M	W	J	I
S	O	V	E	R	E	I	G	N	T	Y	U	F	G	O	G	C	J	J	Q	Z	W	I	O
C	X	U	S	H	U	M	A	N	I	T	A	R	I	A	N	D	I	P	L	O	M	A	T
O	X	T	Q	B	O	R	D	E	R	E	D	T	D	I	S	A	R	M	A	M	E	N	T
N	G	F	W	O	F	N	Y	X	C	P	A	R	E	G	I	O	N	A	L	B	L	O	C
T	E	J	C	A	P	I	T	A	L	N	E	G	O	T	I	A	T	I	O	N	S	E	L
R	H	A	Y	Y	G	A	R	I	D	F	H	N	A	T	I	O	N	S	T	A	T	E	B
O	S	B	L	I	P	S	E	E	L	U	F	K	U	E	M	B	A	S	S	Y	R	U	X
L	A	T	B	L	M	F	T	R	A	D	E	T	E	R	R	E	N	C	E	F	U	W	P
E	N	I	N	R	I	I	M	P	E	R	I	A	L	I	S	M	T	R	E	A	T	Y	D
M	C	E	A	F	N	A	T	I	O	N	A	L	I	N	T	E	R	E	S	T	J	D	E
B	T	G	X	U	B	G	N	N	G	L	O	B	A	L	I	Z	A	T	I	O	N	U	D
A	I	T	M	L	F	T	O	C	B	V	F	O	R	E	I	G	N	P	O	L	I	C	Y
R	O	G	O	V	E	R	N	M	E	N	T	R	E	C	I	P	R	O	C	I	T	Y	D
G	N	I	R	I	D	Z	E	C	O	O	P	E	R	A	T	I	O	N	O	E	P	G	S
O	S	D	O	M	E	S	T	I	C	P	O	L	I	C	Y	H	E	G	E	M	O	N	Z

alliance
ambassador
arms control
arms race
border
capital
collective security
cooperation
deterrence
diplomat
disarmament
domestic policy
embargo
embassy
foreign policy
globalization
government
hegemon
humanitarian
imperialism
multinational
nation-state
national interest
negotiations
NGO
reciprocity
regional bloc
sanctions
sovereignty
trade
treaty
United Nations

Word paths: International relations *Find and circle the secret words below by following a connected path through the maze. Some words may overlap.*

A	M	B	G	B	A	R	U	A	L	L
N		A		M		G		R		I
A	S	S	B	E	O	O	A	M	S	E
D		T		T		D		S		E
O	R	D	E	R	A	D	E	R	A	C
B										N
O	R	E	I	P		R	A	T	I	O
F		I		L		E		A		T
T	N	G	C	O	O	P	O	N	M	N
R		Y		A		C		Y		E
E	A	T	D	I	S	A	R	M	A	M

1. Exchange of goods between countries. _ _ _ _ _
2. An agreement between countries. _ _ _ _ _ _
3. Countries that fight on the same side. _ _ _ _ _ _
4. A competition to build powerful weapons. _ _ _ _ _ _ _ _
5. An important diplomat. _ _ _ _ _ _ _ _ _ _
6. A prohibition of trade. _ _ _ _ _ _ _
7. The line that divides countries. _ _ _ _ _ _
8. A reduction of weapons. _ _ _ _ _ _ _ _ _ _ _
9. Working together. _ _ _ _ _ _ _ _ _ _ _
10. Another word for country. _ _ _ _ _ _
11. From another country. _ _ _ _ _ _ _

Hidden message: International relations *Use the remaining letters to uncover an idiom related to international relations.*

Using military threats to get what you want:

_ _ _ _ _ _ _   _ _ _ _ _ _ _ _ _

Human conflict

·18·

VOCABULARY

ambush
armistice
arms
artillery
belligerent
blockade
border dispute
casualties
civil war
civilian
collateral damage
combatant
conflict
crisis
death toll
drone
espionage
front line
Geneva conventions
guerrillas
hostilities
infantry
minefield
navy
peace treaty
peacekeepers
preemptive strike
raid
rebels
refugees
siege
surrender
troops
truce

PUZZLE 18·1

Definition match-up: Human conflict *Match the following definitions with words from the vocabulary list.*

1. Fighting (in general): ____________________
2. Fighting within a country: ____________________
3. Warlike, hostile, or aggressive: ____________________
4. A place where fighting is occurring: ____________________
5. The surrounding and attacking of a city: ____________________
6. People wounded or killed during hostilities: ____________________
7. People who have fled war zones: ____________________
8. The number of people killed in a conflict: ____________________
9. Unintended destruction caused by war: ____________________
10. The act of spying: ____________________
11. Soldiers that fight on the ground (on foot): ____________________
12. An unmanned robotic aircraft: ____________________
13. Weapons that fire explosives long distances: ____________________

14. An area with buried explosives that go off when stepped on: ________________

15. A time of emergency: ________________

16. A conflict because two nations claim the same territory: ________________

17. Someone who engages in fighting: ________________

18. A permanent cessation of hostilities: ________________

19. An irregular group of combatants: ________________

20. Combatants who are fighting against their government: ________________

21. Lay down your arms and give up fighting: ________________

22. The branch of the military that fights on the seas and oceans: ________________

23. A temporary cessation of hostilities: ________________

24. A series of treaties that protect noncombatants and prisoners of war: ________________

PUZZLE

18·2

Labeling: Human conflict *Attach the following conflict-related labels to the lists of words below.*

Branches of the military	Cessation of hostilities	Noncombatants
Casualties	Munitions	Types of attack

1. armistice, peace treaty ________________
2. ambush, raid ________________
3. landmines, missiles ________________
4. civilians, medical personnel ________________
5. killed, wounded ________________
6. air force, marines ________________

Fill in the blanks: Human conflict *Complete the following paragraphs by filling in the blanks using the words provided.*

Arms control

biological	civilians	landmines	munitions
children	destructiveness	maiming	poison

There are many ways that lawmakers have tried to limit the ______________ of war by limiting the combatants and the ______________ that combatants use. For example, most nations of the world prohibit the use of ______________ as soldiers and prohibit attacks on ______________. Munitions such as ______________ gas and ______________ agents are also banned by international treaty. In recent years, many activists have tried to ban the use of ______________ as well because they stay in the ground, killing or ______________ unsuspecting civilians long after the conflict is over.

Words used to describe conflict

ambush	describe	preemptive	sabotage
blockade	espionage	raid	siege

There are many words used to ______________ hostilities among combatants. For example, a ______________ is when an army surrounds a city or fortified area and slowly wears down the defenses using artillery. A ______________ is a short, quick attack with limited objectives. An ______________ is when soldiers hide and then surprise enemies who pass by. A ______________ strike is when a country attacks another country in order to prevent the other country from attacking first. Not all belligerent actions involve fighting, however. ______________, which is the gathering of secret information, can be vital for an army's success. ______________ of an enemy's bridges, roads, and communications can prevent an enemy from fighting effectively. Finally, a ______________ can prevent an enemy from obtaining vital war materials

Geneva conventions

civilians	prisoners	torture	treatment
limit	property	treaties	wounded

The Geneva conventions are a series of international ______________ that attempt to ______________ the destructiveness of war. The Geneva conventions protect noncombatants such as ______________ and medical personnel. They also protect ______________ of war and soldiers ______________ in war. For example, the Geneva conventions forbid the ______________ of prisoners of war in order to obtain information. As well, countries who capture wounded soldiers are obligated to provide them with medical ______________. The Geneva conventions even prohibit the unnecessary destruction of ______________.

Cessation of hostilities

Armistice	chemical	relief
ceasefire	combatants	toll
cessation	optimism	trench

In many countries of the world November 11 is ____________ Day (Veteran's Day in America), which celebrates the ____________ of hostilities of World War I. When the ____________ went into effect, Europe breathed a collective sigh of ____________ as the war was finally over. Though many ____________ went into the war with a sense of ____________, that quickly changed as the death ____________ increased and the horrors of ____________ warfare became apparent. World War I also saw the first widespread use of ____________ weapons such as mustard gas.

PUZZLE 18·4

Crossword: Human conflict

Across

2. A permanent cessation of hostilities.
4. The place where two armies face each other: the ______ line.
9. Unintended destruction: ______ damage.
10. A temporary cessation of hostilities.
12. A branch of the military responsible for protecting a nation's seas.
14. An attack meant to prevent another country from attacking first: ______ strike.
15. War between factions within a country: ______ war.
16. A small, irregular force of combatants.
20. Tanks and other mobile weapons.
22. An attack made by soldiers who are hiding.
24. Missiles, shells, and land mines.
25. Using force to prevent people or materials from going into an area.
26. A person who has been forced to flee from hostilities.
27. Hostile or aggressive.

Down

1. Soldiers who fight on foot.
3. A person who is engaged in fighting.
5. The number of people killed in fighting: death ______.
6. The branch of the military responsible for guarding a nation's air space.
7. Soldiers whose job it is to maintain the peace by keeping combatants apart.
8. An explosive that blows up when stepped on.
10. Weapons that fire explosive shells over distances.
11. An attack on a city in which the city is surrounded and bombarded over a period of time.
13. A short attack with limited objectives.
15. A person who is killed or injured during hostilities.
17. Lay down your arms and quit fighting.
18. The act of spying or intelligence gathering.
19. The destruction of bridges, railroads, or communications by agents behind enemy lines.
21. The P in POW.
23. A robotic aircraft.

Word search: Human conflict *Find the following words in the grid.*

L	A	N	D	M	I	N	E	W	O	U	N	D	E	D	B	A	L	L	I	A	N	C	E
Q	L	A	O	P	S	U	R	R	E	N	D	E	R	I	C	O	N	F	L	I	C	T	S
T	R	U	C	E	G	U	E	R	R	I	L	L	A	S	V	Y	M	R	N	E	K	E	W
Y	P	D	I	A	C	Y	B	D	T	N	S	Y	E	R	M	G	I	B	V	T	N	J	Y
L	R	O	S	C	O	V	E	Z	P	E	W	E	A	R	Z	L	S	I	E	I	S	H	W
A	A	D	D	E	L	H	L	C	G	N	G	W	A	Z	Q	N	T	E	R	R	A	P	Y
R	U	O	E	K	D	M	S	E	R	U	L	E	M	R	O	P	R	A	S	A	G	Q	M
M	S	A	V	E	W	K	I	L	F	I	N	W	G	I	M	I	M	E	Q	Q	E	S	H
I	Q	I	A	E	A	S	F	E	V	I	S	L	T	E	F	O	I	Y	N	D	E	X	I
S	C	R	S	P	R	P	R	I	L	X	L	I	E	E	N	T	R	A	A	I	E	Z	J
T	O	F	T	I	M	C	C	T	S	O	N	R	S	G	I	E	I	K	T	G	E	Z	D
I	M	O	A	N	O	Q	N	P	T	U	P	A	A	L	L	L	C	L	A	L	M	A	D
C	B	R	T	G	Y	O	O	H	M	Z	E	V	I	L	I	O	A	N	I	Z	S	R	E
E	A	C	I	Q	R	O	T	I	W	C	A	T	I	V	L	U	O	S	E	A	B	U	M
N	T	E	O	F	R	A	G	P	O	P	S	T	I	B	S	I	S	O	Z	E	C	Z	K
A	A	A	N	T	E	L	K	O	Y	O	R	C	D	A	P	I	E	T	R	D	G	O	P
V	N	I	N	D	R	O	N	E	H	A	I	H	C	S	M	D	I	S	P	U	T	E	F
Y	T	W	K	K	T	P	Q	E	N	S	A	B	E	R	R	A	T	T	L	I	N	G	O

air force
alliance
allies
armistice
armor
army
artillery
blockade
bomber
casualties
ceasefire
civil war
civilian
cold war
combatant
conflict
crisis
death toll
devastation
dispute
drone
espionage
front line
guerrilla
hostilities
land mine
marines
missile
munitions
navy
peacekeeping
preemptive
rebels
refugees
saber rattling
siege
surrender
tank
troops
truce
wounded

Describing materials and objects

VOCABULARY

abrasive
audible
brittle
coarse
colossal
corrosive
dull
durable
firm
flexible
flimsy
fragile
harmless
hazardous
hollow
lethal
massive
microscopic
miniature
miniscule
opaque
portable
rough
sharp
smooth
sturdy
symmetrical
tangible
toxic
transparent
versatile
visible

PUZZLE **19·1**

Definition match-up: Describing materials and objects

Match the following definitions with words from the vocabulary list. More than one word may fit some of the definitions.

1. Can be heard: ____________________
2. Easy to break: ____________________
3. See-through: ____________________
4. Huge: ____________________
5. Can eat away at metal or other materials: ____________________
6. Nothing on the inside: ____________________
7. Can be touched: ____________________
8. Very useful: ____________________
9. Deadly: ____________________
10. Tiny: ____________________
11. Has two sides that are mirror images: ____________________

12. Safe: ______________

13. Can be bent: ______________

14. Can be carried: ______________

PUZZLE
19·2

Word sort: Positive or negative? *If the following words were describing a consumer good, would they most likely be positive or negative?*

brittle	flimsy	sturdy
bulky	lightweight	toxic
durable	portable	

POSITIVE		NEGATIVE	
______	______	______	______
______	______	______	______

PUZZLE
19·3

Labeling: Describing materials and objects *Attach the following labels to the lists of adjectives below.*

Clear	Large	Potentially harmful
Easy to bend or stretch	Not clear	Rough textures
Easy to break	Not easy to bend or stretch	Small

1. colossal, immense, massive ______________
2. microscopic, miniature, miniscule ______________
3. cloudy, murky, opaque ______________
4. abrasive, coarse, gritty ______________
5. brittle, flimsy, fragile ______________
6. corrosive, noxious, toxic ______________
7. elastic, flexible, pliable ______________
8. firm, rigid, stiff ______________
9. see-through, translucent, transparent ______________

Fill in the blanks: Describing materials and objects *Complete the following paragraphs by filling in the blanks using the words provided.*

Transparent materials

filter	murky	through
glasses	opaque	transmits
light	shadows	transparent

Some materials allow ______________ to pass ______________ them, and some materials block light. If a material ______________ light, we say that it is see-through or ______________. Windows and ______________ are examples of transparent objects. If a material blocks light, we say that it is ______________. Opaque materials create ______________ behind them when lights shine on them. If a liquid is opaque, we say that it is cloudy or ______________. A ______________ is a tool that allows some colors of light to pass through but blocks other colors of light from passing through.

Hazardous materials

chemicals	dispose	noxious
contaminating	health	regulations
corrosive	lethal	transported

Many materials that people use are hazardous to their ______________. Acids, for example, are ______________ and can eat away at skin, metal, and other materials. Other materials can give off ______________ fumes that can make people sick. Some materials are even ______________ in high doses and could kill people. As such, most countries have strong ______________ for handling hazardous materials. In particular, when hazardous materials are ______________ through towns or cities, there are very strict laws that ensure the safety of people should an accident occur. As well, when companies ______________ of hazardous wastes, regulations try to prevent toxic ______________ from leaking into the environment. Even with strong regulations, however, there have been many cases of toxic chemicals ______________ the soil and groundwater.

Portable goods

bulky	durable	portable	size
compact	lightweight	producers	

______________ goods are goods that people can carry around with them. When making portable goods, ______________ need to consider two things: weight and ______________. Portable goods should be ______________ so that people can lift them even if they are not strong. Portable goods should also be ______________ so that they can fit into most spaces. If an object is ____________, it may be hard to carry around even if it is lightweight. And of course, like all consumer goods, they should be ____________ so that they last a long time.

Plastic

containers	plastic	sturdy
lightweight	pliable	versatile
mold	shatter	waterproof

____________ is used to produce countless consumer goods, making it one of the most ____________ materials ever created. It is ____________, which makes it easy to shape and ____________. It is ____________ so it doesn't break easily. It is ____________ so it can be used to make ____________ for liquids. And unlike glass, it won't ____________ into a million pieces if you drop it. It is also ____________, which makes it easy to carry.

PUZZLE 19·5

Keyword clues: Describing materials and objects *Use the keywords to identify the materials. The simile clues at the end can give you extra hints to solve the puzzle.*

1. _ _ _ _ _ (3 under letter 2)	transparent, fragile, versatile, rigid, used in windows
2. _ _ _ _ _ _ _ (21 under letter 1, 16 under letter 2, 11 under letter 7)	lightweight, sturdy, flexible, waterproof, extremely versatile, used in toys
3. _ _ _ _ (2 under letter 2, 27 under letter 3)	valuable, malleable, metallic, dense, used in jewelry
4. _ _ _ _ (18 under letter 3, 12 under letter 4)	smooth, shiny, lightweight, used in clothes
5. _ _ _ _ _ _ (6 under letter 1, 20 under letter 3, 7 under letter 5)	ductile, malleable, shiny, metallic, used in wires
6. _ _ _ _ (14 under letter 2)	rigid, opaque, flammable, versatile, used in furniture
7. _ _ _ _ _ _ (23 under letter 1, 25 under letter 5)	extremely flexible, opaque, used in shoes, hoses, and tires
8. _ _ _ _ _ _ _ (4 under letter 1, 10 under letter 3)	extremely valuable, transparent, rigid, used in jewelry and drills

9. _ _ _ _ _ _ (17 26)	dense, sturdy, rigid, durable, metallic, used in ships and buildings
10. _ _ _ _ _ _ _ _ (22 1 24)	liquid, opaque, metallic, dense, once used in thermometers
11. _ _ _ _ _ (15 5)	corrosive, liquid, hazardous, used to dissolve things
12. _ _ _ _ _ _ _ _ _ _ _ _ (13 8)	lightweight, flimsy, flammable, used in boxes
13. _ _ _ _ _ _ _ _ _ _ (9 19)	lightweight, metallic, shiny, sturdy, used in cans

Similes clues: *Use these similes to help solve the materials above.*

Simile 1

Freezing:

as _ _ _ _ (1 2 3 4) as _ _ _ (5 6 7)

Simile 2

Completely without color:

as _ _ _ _ _ (8 9 10 11 12) as _ _ _ _ (13 14 15 16)

Simile 3

Hard to grab:

as _ _ _ _ _ _ _ _ (17 18 19 20 21 22 23 24) as an _ _ _ (25 26 27)

PUZZLE
19·6

Word paths: Describing objects *Find and circle the secret words below by following a connected path through the maze. Some words may overlap.*

A	F	L	S	E	L	T	E	V	I	S
S		E		L		T		V		S
T	O	X	I	B	R	I	S	I	M	A
U		I		C		B		L		E
R	E	C	Y	D	A	L	E	I	B	L
D		D		U		U		D		V
Y	P	R	W	O	L	C	R	U	A	E
A		A		L		S		S		R
R	A	H	O	L	M	I	N	I	M	S
M		S		U		A		E		A
L	E	S	E	R	U	T	D	L	I	T

1. Useful in many ways. _ _ _ _ _ _ _ _ _ _
2. Won't hurt you. _
3. Huge. _ _ _ _ _ _ _
4. Not soft. Firm like a rock. _ _ _ _
5. Not dull. Like a knife. _ _ _ _ _
6. Crumbles and breaks easily. _ _ _ _ _ _ _
7. Very small scale. _ _ _ _ _ _ _ _ _
8. Also very small scale. _ _ _ _ _ _ _ _ _
9. Can be bent without breaking. _ _ _ _ _ _ _ _
10. Strong. _ _ _ _ _ _
11. Poisonous or noxious. _ _ _ _ _
12. Empty inside. _ _ _ _ _ _
13. Opaque or murky (like a liquid). _ _ _ _ _ _
14. Can be heard. _ _ _ _ _ _ _
15. Can be seen. _ _ _ _ _ _ _

Hidden message: Describing objects *Use the remaining letters to uncover an idiom about transparency.*

Completely opaque:

__ ______ __ ___

PUZZLE 19·7

Word scramble: Describing materials and objects *Use the clues on the left to unscramble the letters and form words used to describe materials and objects.*

1. Occupies a lot of space:	K L B Y U	_ _ _ _ _ (18, 26)
2. Poisonous or harmful:	X O I T C	_ _ _ _ _ (1)
3. Easily carried:	A B P O T R E L	_ _ _ _ _ _ _ _ (8)
4. Can kill you:	T H A L L E	_ _ _ _ _ _ (6, 9)
5. Lets light pass through:	P A R T E T R S N A N	_ _ _ _ _ _ _ _ _ _ _ (4, 16)
6. Breaks easily:	G R A F E L I	_ _ _ _ _ _ _ (25, 14)
7. Can be seen:	B L E S I I V	_ _ _ _ _ _ _ (22, 7)
8. Large in size or weight:	S A M V I S E	_ _ _ _ _ _ _ (15, 27)
9. Can be touched:	A N G T L E B I	_ _ _ _ _ _ _ _ (17, 20)
10. Not flexible:	G R I D I	_ _ _ _ _ (5, 12)
11. Lasts a long time:	R U D A L E B	_ _ _ _ _ _ _ (21, 24)
12. Can be used in many ways:	T I L E S A E R V	_ _ _ _ _ _ _ _ _ (3, 11)
13. Does not transmit light:	Q U O P A E	_ _ _ _ _ _ (10, 19)
14. Empty inside:	L O H O W L	_ _ _ _ _ _ (2)
15. Dissolves things like an acid:	R O V S I E R O C	_ _ _ _ _ _ _ _ _ (13, 23)

PUZZLE
19·8

Code breaker *Use the number code in Puzzle 19•7 to solve the proverb.*

The importance of being flexible:

_ _ _   _ _ _ _   _ _ _ _   _ _ _ _ _'_   _ _ _ _   _ _ _ _ _ _.

1 2 3   4 5 6 7   8 9 10 11   12 13 14 15 16 17   18 19 20 21   22 23 24 25 26 27

PUZZLE
19·9

Crossword: Describing objects

Across

5. Can be heard.
6. Easy to stretch.
8. Not flexible.
11. Useful.
14. Opaque like a liquid.
15. The opposite of sharp.
17. Empty inside.
19. See-through.
22. Can't be seen with the naked eye.
24. Deadly.
26. Tiny.

Down

1. Huge.
2. Rough in texture.
3. Easy to break.
4. Occupies much volume.
7. Weak and easy to break.
9. Long lasting.
10. Dangerous.
12. Extremely large.
13. Not rough.
16. Dissolves, like acid.
18. Not dangerous.
20. Can be carried.
21. Can be seen.
23. Blocks light.
25. Poisonous.

Demographic trends

·20·

VOCABULARY

average income
birth rate
children per household
cost of living
debt burden
divorce rate
early retirement
environmental awareness
extended family
household
industrialization
infant mortality rate
inflation
life expectancy
literacy rate
materialism
middle class
nuclear family
population
poverty line
quality of life
single-parent household
standard of living
unemployment rate
urbanization

PUZZLE 20·1

Definition match-up: Demographic trends *Match the following definitions with words from the vocabulary list.*

1. A family living under one roof: ______________________
2. Family with two parents plus their children: ______________________
3. Several generations under one roof: ______________________
4. Family with only one parent: ______________________
5. Number of people who can read: ______________________
6. The development of industry on a large scale: ______________________
7. People who are not rich or poor: ______________________
8. The number of people not working: ______________________
9. The amount of money someone owes: ______________________
10. The desire to have objects: ______________________
11. The number of babies that die in the first year: ______________________
12. How long people live: ______________________
13. The number of people in an area: ______________________
14. Migration from country to city: ______________________
15. The material comfort that people enjoy: ______________________
16. How well people live (in terms of happiness): ______________________

17. Retiring before the age of 65: ______________________

18. Concern for environmental issues: ______________________

19. The number of failed marriages: ______________________

20. The price of goods needed to live: ______________________

21. The rise in the cost of living: ______________________

22. The minimum amount of money needed to buy the necessities for living: ______________________

23. The number of people being born: ______________________

PUZZLE

20·2

Word sort: Trends *The following words can be used to describe trends. Choose three words from the list that could be used to describe downward, steady, and upward trends.*

bottomed out	going up	plateaued	slipping
declining	growing	plummeting	soaring
decreasing	increasing	rising	stable
dropping	leveled off	shrinking	steady
falling	on the decline	sinking	surging
going down	on the rise	skyrocketing	unchanged

UPWARD TRENDS	STEADY TRENDS	DOWNWARD TRENDS
______________	______________	______________
______________	______________	______________
______________	______________	______________
______________	______________	______________
______________	______________	______________
______________	______________	______________
______________		______________
______________		______________
		______________
		______________

Fill in the blanks: Demographic trends for the past 200 years *Complete the following paragraphs by filling in the blanks using the words provided.*

The standard of living

consumer	dramatically	middle	standard
developed	economies	poverty	

The last 200 years have seen a remarkable increase in the _____________ of living in many parts of the world. Modern _____________ have produced a variety of _____________ goods that provide us with material comfort. The _____________ class in _____________ countries has increased _____________ during this period. In these countries the number of people living below the _____________ line has plummeted.

Life expectancy

dropped	material	sanitation	substantial
expectancy	mortality	spread	treatments

Along with an increase in _____________ comforts, there has also been a _____________ increase in life _____________. In particular, infant _____________ rates have _____________ sharply as better healthcare spreads throughout society. As well, the _____________ systems of modern cities have significantly reduced the _____________ of disease throughout society. And, to top it off, new medical _____________ are allowing people to survive diseases that were almost certainly fatal in the past.

Population

age	decline	population	rate
case	money	rapidly	

With the dramatic rise in life expectancy, one might expect a substantial increase in _____________ as more people survive till they reach a childbearing _____________. However, this is usually not the _____________, since an increase in the standard of living is accompanied by a _____________ in the birth _____________. As people become wealthier, they have fewer children but invest more time and _____________ into the children they do have. In fact, the countries where population is increasing _____________ are usually the poorer countries of the world.

Education

compulsory	masses	public	skyrocketed
literacy	productive	skilled	

One great achievement of the last 200 years is the introduction of free _____________ education in many parts of the world. Some places have gone even further and made education ______________ at the elementary school level. As a result, ______________ rates have ______________. This in turn has created a ______________ workforce in these countries that is far more ______________ than in countries where the ______________ remain illiterate.

A sustainable lifestyle

adverse	debate	run	technologies
climate	fossil	solve	

In recent years, there has been some ______________ as to whether or not we can maintain this standard of living. For one, materialism has had an extremely ______________ effect on the environment. Our lifestyle is causing ______________ change around the globe. As well, our material comfort has depended on the cheap energy from the once abundant ______________ fuels that may now be starting to ______________ out. However, optimists believe that new ______________ will be developed to ______________ our environmental and energy problems.

PUZZLE

20·4

Word scramble: Demographic trend *Find the words described below within the phrase "Demographic Trend." You can use the letters in any order, but you can only use each letter once.*

DEMOGRAPHIC TREND

HINT: USE THE CODE BREAKER TO THE RIGHT TO HELP YOU SOLVE THE WORDS.

CLUES	ANSWERS	CODE BREAKER
1. A person who tells jokes.	_ _ _ _ _ _ _ _	1 x 2 x 3 x x x
2. Something knights wear.	_ _ _ _ _	4 x x x 5
3. Give to charity.	_ _ _ _ _ _	6 x 7 x 8 x
4. The seed of an oak tree.	_ _ _ _ _	x 9 10 x x
5. Words under a picture.	_ _ _ _ _ _ _	12 x 11 8 x x x
6. A person who shoots a bow.	_ _ _ _ _ _	18 5 x 13 x x
7. A rope made of metal links.	_ _ _ _ _	12 x x x 14
8. A precious gem.	_ _ _ _ _ _ _	3 x x 15 x 29 x
9. A place to grow flowers.	_ _ _ _ _ _	16 x 17 x x 7
10. Another word for theater.	_ _ _ _ _ _	x x 7 x x 20
11. Another word for collect.	_ _ _ _ _ _	16 x x 27 25 x
12. A person who doesn't play fair.	_ _ _ _ _ _ _	9 13 x 18 28 x x
13. Find similarities.	_ _ _ _ _ _ _	19 x 15 11 x x x
14. Something ships transport.	_ _ _ _ _	19 x 21 24 10

15. Another word for respect. _ _ _ _ _ _ 4 22 15 x 17 x

16. Secret letters. _ _ _ _ 23 x 26 x

17. The opposite of arrive. _ _ _ _ _ _ 26 x x 4 x 8

18. A thing to keep ships from drifting. _ _ _ _ _ _ 18 x 1 30 x 21

19. A fire-breathing monster. _ _ _ _ _ _ x 5 x 24 x 14

20. Work to do around the home. _ _ _ _ _ 12 30 x 17 x

21. Another word for winner. _ _ _ _ _ _ _ _ 23 30 x 2 11 x x 29

22. Wear away the land. _ _ _ _ _ 25 x x 6 x

23. A wooden box. _ _ _ _ _ 19 21 x 28 x

24. A round piece of metal money. _ _ _ _ 9 10 x x

25. Think the same thing as someone. _ _ _ _ _ 20 16 x x 25

26. The planet we live on. _ _ _ _ _ x 20 x x 13

27. Try to lose weight. _ _ _ _ 22 x x 28

28. Out of sight. _ _ _ _ _ _ 27 x 6 22 x 14

PUZZLE **20·5**

Word sort: Trend modifiers *The following words can be used to describe trends. Decide if the words can be used to indicate major/large, steady, or minor/insignificant changes.*

consistent	insignificant	sharp	substantial
considerable	marginal	significant	sudden
dramatic	modest	slight	
gradual	negligible	steady	

MAJOR/LARGE CHANGE	STEADY CHANGE	MINOR/INSIGNIFICANT CHANGE
__________	__________	__________
__________	__________	__________
__________	__________	__________
__________	__________	__________

PUZZLE 20·6

Trend modifiers: Changing adjectives to adverbs *Rephrase the following phrases, changing adjectives to adverbs and nouns to verbs. The first one has been done for you.*

1. a gradual increase *increase gradually*
2. a sudden drop: ______________________
3. a sharp decrease: ______________________
4. a dramatic rise: ______________________
5. a marginal decline: ______________________
6. a steady rise: ______________________
7. a modest growth: ______________________
8. a consistent drop: ______________________

PUZZLE 20·7

Crossword: Demographic trends

Across

1. People who have a comfortable standard of living, but are not rich: _______ class.
3. Education for the masses: free _______ education.
5. How much you pay for housing, groceries, clothing, and so on: the _______ of living.
8. The minimum income needed to buy necessities for living: _______ line.
9. The number of people being born: _______ rate.
12. A household with three or more generations living together: _______ family.
16. The development of industry on a large scale.
21. The number of people not working: _______ rate.
23. Movement of people from one area to another in mass.
24. The average life-span: life _______.

Down

2. Decreasing: on the _______.
4. The material wealth of a society: the standard of _______.
6. Increase rapidly.
7. Migration of people to the cities.
8. The number of people living somewhere.
10. A group of people living under a single roof.
11. The number of babies that die in the first year of life: infant _______ rate.
13. A household with only parents and children living together: _______ family.
14. Increasing: on the _______.
15. The number of people who can read: _______ rate.
16. The rise in the price of goods.
17. The number of failed marriages: _______ rate.
18. How well you live: _______ of life.
19. Decrease rapidly.
20. A parent raising children without a spouse: _______ parent.
22. Stop increasing: _______ off.

PUZZLE **20·8**

Collocation match-up: Demographic trends *Match the following words with their collocations below.*

average	bottomed	dramatic	life	poverty	single
birth	debt	leveled	middle	nuclear	standard

1. _______________ expectancy
2. _______________ income
3. _______________ parent
4. _______________ burden

5. ____________ rate

6. ____________ out

7. ____________ increase

8. ____________ of living

9. ____________ off

10. ____________ class

11. ____________ family

12. ____________ line

Word Search: Demographic trends *Find the following words in the grid.*

```
Q L Q H I L U X U T R N U C L E A R F A M I L Y
Z I L D E H J S T A N D A R D O F L I V I N G J
T F C O N S I D E R A B L E K U B P T S H Y T Y
J E U F K S R C O H C T R I X I O S P O E Z I D
V E B O C Z J M U P S A P Z O R N L H C C G K H
M X D E C L I N E L O U X O D I G I X A G U N C
I P U S A M O D E S T G B Z V A R G E W R X R Y
D E N V I G I L L P G M D S U E G H B X H P C P
D C E Y E N V N E P O D P Y T G R T I D K A J C
L T M B V C G M C L V P X A Y A T T E C R K I J
E A P F I Y G L G O E Q U Q C E N S Y E K T A E
C N L P A R S I E R M G A L K E A T T L A G S G
L C O L P N T Z F P A E R C A E E I I M I A X Z
A Y Y U M J M H B B A D O O R T L X A A E N Y H
S V M M R O N U R K Y R U C W F I R T R L N E B
S N E M K J H P S A Y L E A X A D O C P A D U O
O R N E C L I M B K T D E N L L X N N N G L X P
W B T T C J B B S E D E T E T L I D I V O R C E
```

birth rate
climb
considerable
decline
decrease
divorce
dramatic
drop
fall
gradual
grow
income
increase
life expectancy
literacy
middle class
modest
nuclear family
plummet
population
poverty line
rise
sharp
single parent
skyrocket
slight
soar
standard of living
substantial
unemployment

Theory and research

·21·

VOCABULARY

absurd
accurate
conjecture
ambiguous
anomaly
assert
causal relation
claim
conjecture
contradict
correlation
data
debate
debunk
disprove
dubious
empirical
enigma
extrapolate
fallacy
hypothesis
misconception
objective
paradigm
paradox
phenomena
plausible
proof
refute
sample size
scrutinize
speculate
unbiased

PUZZLE 21·1

Definition match-up: Theory and research *Match the following definitions with words from the vocabulary list. More than one word may fit some of the definitions.*

1. Show that something is not true: ____________________
2. Seems reasonable or possibly true: ____________________
3. Unlikely to be true: ____________________
4. An apparent contradiction: ____________________
5. Things that happen in the natural world: ____________________
6. A belief that is not true: ____________________
7. Argue about the truth: ____________________
8. Something puzzling or difficult to understand: ____________________
9. A guess: ____________________
10. Make a guess: ____________________
11. A model of reality: ____________________

12. Predict what will happen based on a trend: ____________________

13. Based on observation or experience: ____________________

14. The number of observations: ____________________

PUZZLE **21·2**

Collocation match-up: Theory and research *Match the following words with their collocations.*

causal	design	formulate	peer
common	empirical	paradigm	scientific

1. ______ relationship
2. ______ evidence
3. ______ an experiment
4. ______ method
5. ______ misconception
6. ______ review
7. ______ a hypothesis
8. ______ shift

PUZZLE **21·3**

Labeling: Theory and research *Attach the following labels to the lists of words below.*

Doubtful
Empirical evidence
How phenomena are connected
Mistaken beliefs
Natural phenomena
Possibly true
Speculate
State that something is true
The scientific method

1. causal relation, correlation, independent ____________________
2. measurements from a scale, observations from a microscope, temperature readings ____________________
3. earthquakes, reflection of light, sound echoes ____________________
4. errors, fallacies, misconceptions ____________________
5. formulate a hypothesis, design an experiment, gather empirical evidence ____________________
6. argue, assert, claim ____________________
7. dubious, far-fetched, questionable ____________________
8. believable, plausible, reasonable ____________________
9. surmise, hypothesize, theorize ____________________

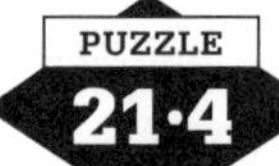

Fill in the blanks: Context *Use the context to choose the correct word out of the four given for the blank.*

1. Scientists use ______ evidence to support their claims.

   theoretical hypothesis empirical anomaly

2. The debate has died down as several recent studies seem to ______ the hypothesis.

   assert claim scrutinize disprove

3. Although the hypothesis was ______, nobody was able to prove it.

   plausible ambiguous absurd accurate

4. Scientists are no longer as certain as they were, since new research seems to ______ the previous results.

   accurate assert prove contradict

5. The data showed that there was an ______ that could not be explained by current theory.

   ambiguous anomaly object data

6. Researchers believe there is a ______ between stress and longevity.

   proof conjecture debate correlation

7. Some scientists ______ that there might be life on other planets.

   anomaly speculate contradict dubious

8. The results were ______, neither proving nor disproving the theory.

   ambiguous contradiction decisive absurd

9. Studies undergo peer review by scientists who ______ the data before the studies are published.

   contradict disprove scrutinize accurate

10. Researchers have found strong evidence to the contrary, thus disproving the ______.

    anomaly conjecture fallacy results

11. The object in the photo was an ______ that baffled scientists everywhere.

    assertion absurd enigma empirical

12. If we ______ from current data, we can predict African elephants will be extinct by 2030.

    extrapolate disprove refute claim

PUZZLE
21·5

Idiom puzzle: Theory and research *Complete the following phrases. Use the symbols below the blanks to help you solve the idioms. Each symbol represents one letter.*

1. Why something occurred: _ _ _ _ _ AND EFFECT
   26 ♥ 31 ♦ ■
2. Repeatedly occurring together: STATISTICAL _ _ _ _ _ _ _ _ _ _ _
   29 ♠ ★ ★ ■ 10 ♥ ◐ ▣ ♠ ▼
3. The number of people surveyed: _ _ _ _ _ _ SIZE
   ♦ 8 ♣ Δ 30 ■
4. The way science is conducted: SCIENTIFIC _ _ _ _ _ _
   ♣ ■ 4 14 ♠ ▲
5. A new scientific model: PARADIGM _ _ _ _ _
   ♦ 1 ▣ 13
6. Other scientists checking your work: _ _ _ _ REVIEW
   Δ 6 ■ ★
7. Make a conjecture: FORMULATE A _ _ _ _ _ _ _ _ _ _
   Δ 25 ◐ 16 ■ ♦ ▣ ♦
8. Data acquired through observation: _ _ _ _ _ _ _ _ _ EVIDENCE
   ■ 22 Δ ▣ ★ ▣ Ω ♥ ●
9. A widely held belief that is wrong: A COMMON _ _ _ _ _ _ _ _ _ _ _ _ _
   ♣ ▣ ♦ Ω 27 7 Ω ■ Δ ◐ ▣ ♠ 35
10. A place to publish research results: A SCIENTIFIC _ _ _ _ _ _ _
    20 ♠ 21 ★ ▼ ♥ ●
11. What happens around us: NATURAL _ _ _ _ _ _ _ _ _
    Δ 5 15 ▼ ♠ ♣ ■ ▼ ♥
12. A paradox: AN APPARENT _ _ _ _ _ _ _ _ _ _ _ _ _
    Ω 11 ▼ ◐ ★ ♥ ▲ 33 Ω ◐ ▣ ♠ ▼
13. Collect data: GATHER _ _ _ _ _ _ _ _
    ■ ♪ 2 ▲ ■ 28 Ω ■
14. Use a microscope: MAKE AN _ _ _ _ _ _ _ _ _ _ _
    ♠ 32 ■ ★ ♪ 18 ◐ ▣ ♠ 12
15. A good argument: A VALID _ _ _ _ _
    Δ 34 ▣ ▼ 24
16. Test a hypothesis: CONDUCT AN _ _ _ _ _ _ _ _ _ _
    ■ Δ ■ ★ 9 ♣ ■ ▼ 3
17. Write down observations: _ _ _ _ _ _ DATA
    ★ 17 Ω ♠ ★ 19
18. Find evidence to the contrary: _ _ _ _ _ _ _ _ A THEORY
    ▲ ▣ 36 23 ★ ♠ ♪ ■

PUZZLE 21·6

Code breaker: Two idioms *Use the number code in Puzzle 21•6 to solve the idioms below.*

Idiom 1

State exactly what the problem is:

_ _ _   _ _ _   _ _ _ _   _ _   _ _ _   _ _ _ _
1 2 3   4 5 6   7 8 9 10   11 12   13 14 15   16 17 18 19

Idiom 2

Judge something without gathering enough evidence:

_ _ _ _   _ _   _ _ _ _ _ _ _ _ _ _ _
20 21 22 23   24 25   26 27 28 29 30 31 32 33 34 35 36

Fill in the blanks: Theory and research *Complete the following paragraphs by filling in the blanks using the words provided.*

The scientific method

empirical	hypotheses	observation	phenomena	verified
experiments	method	peer	reproduce	

The scientific __________ is the way in which scientists investigate natural __________ and develop theories of nature. Scientists formulate __________ about nature and then design __________ to test these hypotheses. The scientific method depends upon the collection of __________ evidence acquired through systematic __________. Any results and conclusions must undergo __________ review. Further, any experiments or observations must be __________ independently. In other words, other scientists must be able to __________ the results of experiments.

Paradigm shifts

anomaly	history	modified	revolution
explained	model	observations	shift

A paradigm is a theoretical __________ of natural phenomena. In normal science, paradigms are constantly being __________ to accommodate new data and __________. However, throughout __________, there have been times when a paradigm has been unable to accommodate new data and observations. In this case, a scientific __________ may occur, resulting in a paradigm ______________, which is the replacement of an old paradigm with a completely new paradigm. These paradigm shifts often come about because of the discovery of an ______________ that cannot be ______________ by the current model.

Cause and effect versus correlation

case	coincidence	depends	necessarily
causes	correlation	fallacy	statistical

When two phenomena, A and B, happen to occur together, it may be just a ______________. However, if the two phenomena repeatedly occur together, we say there is a ______________ between A and B. One common ______________ is to assume that A ______________ B to occur if there is a ______________ correlation between A and B. However, this is not ______________ true. It could be that B causes A to occur or that a third phenomenon, C, causes both A and B to occur. It could even be the case that A and B cause each other to occur. Take for example the ______________ of predator and prey. The number of prey ______________ on the number of predators, while at the same time the number of predators depends on the number of prey.

Paradoxes

according	conclude	critical	paradox	replaced
assume	contradiction	other	puzzles	

A ______________ is a statement that apparently contradicts itself. Many paradoxes are thought ______________ that are useful for teaching ______________ thinking skills. One famous paradox is the liar's paradox, which is as follows: A liar says to you, "What I am telling you is false." Is he lying or not? If we ______________ he is lying, then his statement is true. Therefore, we can ______________ he is not lying, which is a ______________. On the ______________ hand, if we assume he is telling the truth, then ______________ to his statement he must be lying, which is also a contradiction. Another famous paradox is the ship of Theseus, which asks the following question: If a ship is repaired over time so that eventually every piece of wood is ______________, is it the same ship?

PUZZLE 21·8

Word paths: Theory and research

Find and circle the secret words below by following a connected path through the maze. Some words may overlap.

M	P	I	P	P	P	A	R	A	D	O
E		R		H		F		U		X
A	C	I	S	E	N	O	M	E	N	A
L		S		F		O		T		S
H	T	E	T	A	W	R	P	R	E	S
Y		H		L		Y		O		A
P	O	T	N	L	A	C	D	T	U	F
T		W		O		T		E		E
O	G	D	A	T	A	E	T	X	T	R
S		H		E		E		R		A
P	E	C	U	L	A	T	A	L	O	P

1. Predict something based on a trend. __ __ __ __ __ __ __ __ __ __ __
2. The type of evidence researchers gather. __ __ __ __ __ __ __ __ __
3. A misconception. __ __ __ __ __ __ __
4. Things that happen in nature. __ __ __ __ __ __ __ __ __
5. An apparent contradiction. __ __ __ __ __ __ __
6. Research results. __ __ __ __
7. An idea or theory that is not proven. __ __ __ __ __ __ __ __ __ __
8. Make a guess. __ __ __ __ __ __ __ __ __
9. Claim that something is true. __ __ __ __ __ __
10. Argue against something. __ __ __ __ __ __
11. Evidence or arguments that something is true. __ __ __ __ __

Hidden message *Use the remaining letters to uncover an idiom related to uncovering the truth.*

Use the evidence to figure out what happened:

__ __

Crossword: Theory and research

Across

1. Another word for hypothesis.
4. Having other experts scrutinize your results: _______ review.
7. Research results.
9. Something that cannot be explained by current theory.
10. Possibly true.
11. An erroneous belief.
15. A scientific revolution: a paradigm _______.
17. Evidence and arguments that something is true.
19. Open to more than one interpretation.
23. Predict something based on a trend in the data.

Down

2. Refute.
3. Unlikely to be true.
4. A seeming contradiction.
5. State that something is true.
6. State that something is true.
8. Argue.
12. Evidence based on observations and experience.
13. A theory or idea that has yet to be proven.
14. Guess or predict.
16. Ridiculous.
18. An erroneous belief.
20. A model of nature.

Across

24. Examine something very carefully.
25. Things that happen in nature that scientists study.

Down

21. Formulate hypotheses and design experiments to test the hypotheses: the scientific ______.
22. Argue against something

Word scramble: Theory and research *Use the clues on the left to unscramble the letters and form words used to discuss theory and research.*

Clue	Scrambled	Answer
1. Something not explained by a theory:	M A L A N O Y	_ _ _ _ _ _ _ (5, 23)
2. Another word for claim:	T E A S R S	_ _ _ _ _ _ (8, 1)
3. A scientific model:	D I R A P A G M	_ _ _ _ _ _ _ _ (20)
4. Something that baffles you:	N I E M A G	_ _ _ _ _ _ (22, 12)
5. Evidence to show something is true:	O R O F P	_ _ _ _ _ (15, 4)
6. A mistaken argument:	L A F L Y A C	_ _ _ _ _ _ _ (14, 6)
7. Show that something is not true:	R O E V D P I S	_ _ _ _ _ _ _ _ (26, 24)
8. A contradiction:	A R A X O P D	_ _ _ _ _ _ _ (10)
9. Probably not true:	B U D S O U I	_ _ _ _ _ _ _ (9)
10. Something that researchers test:	P Y H O S I S T H E	_ _ _ _ _ _ _ _ _ _ (2, 21)
11. Sunlight, shadows, and tornados:	E N P H E N A O M	_ _ _ _ _ _ _ _ _ (18, 3)
12. Observations:	A T A D	_ _ _ _ (7)
13. A test of a hypothesis:	P E R I E X N E M T	_ _ _ _ _ _ _ _ _ _ (16, 17)
14. A colleague:	R E P E	_ _ _ _ (25, 19)
15. Show that a misconception is not correct:	B K U N D E	_ _ _ _ _ _ (11, 13)

Code breaker *Use the number code in Puzzle 21•9 to solve the phrase below that is related to problems.*

Empirical evidence will reveal the truth.

__ __ __   __ __ __ __ __   __ __ __ __ __   __ __ __   __ __ __ __ __ __ __ __ __ __.
1 2 3   4 5 6 7 8   9 10 11 12 13   14 15 16   17 18 19 20 21 22 23 24 25 26

Answer key

1 Figures of speech

1·1 1. rhyme 2. alliteration 3. simile 4. metaphor 5. hyperbole 6. personification 7. sarcasm 8. onomatopoeia

1·2 1. rhyme 2. alliteration 3. rhyme 4. alliteration 5. alliteration 6. rhyme 7. alliteration 8. rhyme 9. alliteration 10. rhyme 11. rhyme 12. alliteration 13. alliteration 14. rhyme 15. rhyme 16. rhyme 17. alliteration 18. rhyme 19. alliteration 20. alliteration

1·3 1. metaphor 2. personification 3. simile (possible hyperbole) 4. onomatopoeia 5. sarcasm 6. metaphor (possible hyperbole) 7. sarcasm 8. simile 9. personification 10. hyperbole 11. onomatopoeia 12. hyperbole

1·4 **Alliteration and rhyme:** rhyme, speech, repetition, bridges, end, dandy, tear, poems

Simile and metaphor: comparison, as, feather, fish, metaphor, giant, saint

Hyperbole and sarcasm: mean, exaggeration, horse, actually, opposite, accidentally, good

Personification and onomatopoeia: figures, characteristics, leaves, moon, nonliving, crow, bird

1·5 1. swim 2. make 3. copycat 4. about 5. wind 6. merrier 7. brain 8. busy 9. minie 10. slippery 11. gain 12. famine 13. horses 14. silk 15. settle 16. bender 17. dusk 18. snooze 19. common

1·6 make a mountain out of a molehill

1·7 **Across:** 1. bread 4. creepy 6. cold 7. drum 8. flute 10. cry 12. cut 13. easy 15. trick 17. bus 20. east 22. slow 23. candy 25. fog 26. ace 27. busy 30. chocolate 32. common 33. corn 35. look 37. sink 38. ding 39. hand

Down: 1. bear 2. arm 3. flat 4. copy 5. pretty 7. deer 9. eight 11. run 14. strong 16. clean 17. blue 18. stubborn 19. recycle 21. sly 24. dime 25. fossil 28. quick 29. down 31. tick 34. rain 36. old

2 Academic skills

2·1 1. describe 2. compare 3. prove 4. comprehend 5. explain 6. demonstrate 7. research 8. record 9. paraphrase 10. sequence 11. observe 12. measure 13. discuss 14. predict 15. contrast 16. evaluate 17. classify 18. solve 19. summarize

2·2 1. make a comparison 2. find a solution 3. have a discussion 4. give a demonstration 5. do an experiment 6. do research 7. make a prediction 8. give a description 9. take a measurement 10. give an explanation

2·3 1. summarize 2. contrast 3. classify 4. describe 5. compare 6. paraphrase 7. sequence 8. predict

2·4 1. diagram 2. documentary 3. glossary 4. graph

2·5 **Across:** 1. give 4. record 6. paraphrase 7. graph 8. documentary 9. find 10. have 12. comprehend 15. prove 17. make 18. discuss 19. sequence 21. describe 24. predict 26. evaluate 27. summarize 28. table 29. compare

Down: 1. glossary 2. explain 3. measure 4. research 5. do 11. solve 12. classify 13. map 14. demonstrate 16. observe 20. express 22. estimate 23. contrast 25. diagram

2·6

E	V	A	L	U	A	T	E	M	H	E	X	P	E	R	I	M	E	N	T
R	E	W	H	D	S	P	R	E	D	I	C	T	R	E	C	O	R	D	O
E	O	P	E	I	O	E	N	A	U	S	U	M	M	A	R	I	Z	E	S
S	D	C	A	A	L	S	Q	S	N	C	H	M	E	M	O	R	I	Z	E
E	E	O	O	G	V	O	L	U	D	A	I	D	E	N	T	I	F	Y	D
A	S	M	P	R	E	O	O	R	E	R	L	C	O	M	P	A	R	E	T
R	C	P	A	A	C	L	O	E	R	N	S	Y	D	I	S	C	U	S	S
C	R	R	R	M	E	S	A	P	S	R	C	I	Z	S	O	N	A	E	D
H	I	E	A	O	U	C	A	T	T	I	O	E	N	E	I	R	S	T	H
O	B	H	P	E	V	O	R	G	A	N	I	Z	E	C	T	M	O	S	T
B	E	E	H	P	R	E	S	E	N	T	N	P	O	N	R	W	E	R	F
S	U	N	R	L	G	W	E	M	D	A	F	P	O	O	N	E	W	H	I
E	C	D	A	H	R	Y	O	O	U	C	E	C	E	X	P	L	A	I	N
R	A	N	S	U	A	S	E	D	T	O	R	E	S	T	I	M	A	T	E
V	C	H	E	A	P	N	G	E	D	E	M	O	N	S	T	R	A	T	E
E	E	T	H	E	H	W	O	L	R	L	D	C	L	A	S	S	I	F	Y

2·7 **Quotation 1:** He who opens a school door closes a prison.

Quotation 2: Education is the most powerful weapon which you can use to change the world.

2·8 **Problem solving:** solved, find, brainstorm, ideas, creative, outside

Comparison: make, similarities, example, both, contrast, whereas, apple

Classification: sort, characteristics, animals, divided, subgroups, birds

Presenting information: organize, graphs, diagrams, relationship, works, columns, headings

Making an argument: persuade, thesis, supporting, examples, comprehend, summarize

Experiments: experiment, hypothesis, control, observe, data, prove

3 Rules and laws

3·1 1. unbiased, impartial 2. prohibit, forbid, ban, abolish 3. compulsory, mandatory 4. transgress, infringe 5. severe, strict 6. pass, enact 7. obey, comply 8. lenient, lax 9. legal, lawful 10. lawsuit, court case

3·2 1. smoking gun 2. disturb the peace 3. due process 4. false pretenses 5. contempt of court 6. act of god 7. fine print 8. null and void 9. extenuating circumstances 10. burden of proof 11. in good faith 12. paper trail

3·3 1. due process 2. smoking gun 3. burden of proof 4. act of god 5. contempt of court 6. disturb the peace 7. false pretenses 8. extenuating circumstances

3·4 1. Things that people obey 2. Things that are mandatory in some countries 3. Transgressions of the law 4. Principles of justice 5. Severity of punishments 6. Legal responsibility

3·5 **Principles of justice:** disputes, infringed, revenge, hands, sue, principles, fundamental, equality, treatment

Age of majority: rights, adults, majority, minors, allowed, consume, prohibited, lenient

Citizen responsibilities: legal, protect, responsibilities, mandatory, required, oath, military, voluntary

Enforcement: code, function, paper, obey, apprehend, punish, corruption, enforced, lack

The first law codes: codes, Hammurabi's, preserved, tablets, injuring, eye, draconian, penalties, broke

3·6 1. court 2. break 3. burden 4. book 5. down 6. letter 7. smoking 8. clear 9. forbidden 10. nose 11. against 12. crack 13. disturb 14. law-abiding 15. thumb 16. above 17. eyes 18. contempt

3·7 Rules are meant to be broken.

3·8 1. prohibit 2. abolish 3. mandatory 4. severe 5. permit 6. compel 7. repeal 8. penalty 9. illegal 10. enforce 11. lawsuit 12. unbiased 13. ban

Hidden message: a slap on the wrist

3·9 **Across:** 1. permit 4. lawful 5. exempt 7. enact 8. penalty 10. crack 12. compulsory 15. break 19. rule 21. letter 22. obey 24. lawsuit 25. ban 26. liability

Down: 1. proof 2. repeal 3. impartial 4. lax 6. minor 9. forbidden 11. code 12. comply 13. majority 14. sue 16. allowed 17. restrict 18. illegal 20. prohibit 23. law

3·10 1. enact 2. lenient 3. prohibit 4. allow 5. compel 6. severe 7. code 8. abolish 9. obey 10. lawful 11. smoking gun 12. lawsuit 13. impartial 14. ban 15. restrict

3·11 **Idiom 1:** cover your tracks

Idiom 2: blow the whistle

4 Crime and punishment

4·1 1. shoplifting 2. burglary 3. driving intoxicated 4. dealing narcotics 5. possession of narcotics 6. jaywalking 7. blackmail 8. vandalism 9. littering 10. armed robbery 11. speeding 12. perjury 13. assault 14. tax evasion 15. bribery 16. arson

4·2 Answers will vary. Felonies could be armed robbery, arson, blackmail, bribery, dealing narcotics, kidnapping, murder/homicide, perjury, smuggling, tax evasion. Misdemeanors could be arson, assault, jaywalking, littering, pickpocketing, possession of narcotics, public intoxication, shoplifting, speeding, vandalism.

4·3 1. Criminals in general 2. Criminals who steal 3. Verdicts 4. Criminals who destroy property 5. Where criminals are kept 6. Investigation procedures 7. People at a trial 8. Evidence 9. Sentences

4·4

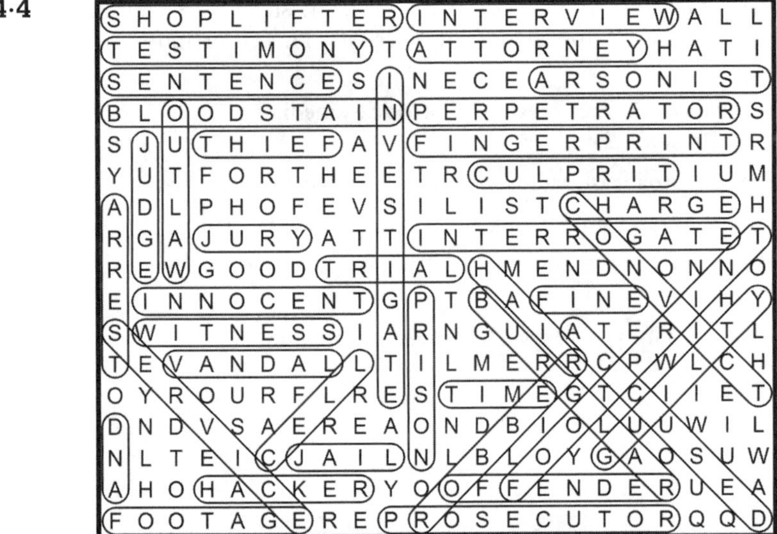

4·5 **Quotation:** All that is necessary for the triumph of evil is that good men do nothing.

Proverb: Tell me who your friends are and I will tell you who you are.

4·6 1. thief 2. burglar 3. vandal 4. shoplifter 5. robber 6. hacker 7. pickpocket 8. pirate 9. culprit 10. bandit

Hidden message: He got caught red-handed.

4·7 **Evidence:** DNA, fingerprints, testimony, bloodstains, surveillance video, gunshot residue, footprints

Procedures: investigate, charge, arrest, interview, interrogate, put on trial, sentence

People involved: witness, the accused, fugitive, the jury, victim, the judge, police officer, prosecutor, detective, suspect

4·8 1. culprit, perpetrator, outlaw, criminal 2. witness 3. detective, police officer 4. jury 5. victim 6. fugitive 7. judge 8. witness, police officer, detective 9. the accused 10. prosecutor

4·9 1. of 2. of 3. for 4. with 5. of 6. for 7. in 8. on 9. to 10. for 11. of

4·10 **Crimes:** against, vandalism, shoplifting, victim, committed, investigation, perpetrator

Investigations: breaks, scene, evidence, witnesses, suspects, interrogate, alibi

Arrests: charge, arrest, resist, fugitives, handcuffs, cell

Trials: trial, accused, jury, testimony, innocent, sentence

Punishment: convicted, felonies, armed, serve, prison, misdemeanors, fine, community

4·11 1. tiger 2. evil 3. cure 4. diet 5. litter 6. give 7. city 8. clue 9. rice 10. dirt 11. turtle 12. true 13. glue 14. duel 15. edit 16. cutlery 17. drive 18. rude 19. girl 20. guide 21. tidy 22. dice 23. rug 24. dry

4·12 **Across:** 4. vandal 5. jury 7. dealer 10. judge 12. police officer 14. court 15. away 17. trial 21. crime 22. interrogate 24. alibi 26. detective 27. perpetrator 31. criminal 32. suspect

Down: 1. fingerprint 2. evidence 3. armed 6. burglar 8. arson 9. felony 11. sentence 13. law 16. arrested 18. bloodstain 19. DNA 20. victim 23. theft 24. assault 25. break 28. prison 29. accuse 30. fine

5 Journalism and mass media

5·1 1. article 2. column 3. editorial 4. exposé 5. coverage 6. broadcast media 7. print media 8. journalist, correspondent 9. headlines 10. front page 11. biased, one-sided 12. objective 13. propaganda 14. spin 15. sensationalist 16. tabloid 17. verify 18. censorship 19. sources 20. press release

5·2 1. Sensationalist media 2. Online media 3. Free press 4. Broadcast media 5. Government-controlled media 6. Print media

5·3 **Types of media:** media, print, newspapers, broadcast, radio, online, professional, blog, quality

Principles of journalism: objective, other, biased, sides, mind, verify, sources, sensationalist

The media as a watchdog: function, watchdog, corruption, inefficiency, eye, polluting, investigative, order, independent

Censorship: aired, censorship, criticism, profanity, free, speech, slander, incite

5·4 **Across:** 1. blog 3. coverage 4. release 5. criticism 7. newspaper 8. source 10. impartial 12. radio 13. correspondent 15. press 18. editorial 23. journalist 24. article 25. slander

Down: 1. broadcast 2. censorship 3. column 6. propaganda 9. anchor 10. independent 11. biased 14. print 16. scandal 17. headline 19. objective 20. tabloid 21. front 22. verify

5·5

```
M M H A X I N T E R V I E W J O U R N A L I S T
G U W M H S K W T P R O P A G A N D A B G J D C
V Q E F A R P S E N S A T I O N A L I S T E U E
Z T V I O I A R V T B Q T I N D E P E N D E N T
B M B W E C N R E P O R T E R O F F E N S I V E
U G T S D I G S K S P R E S S R E L E A S E T D
D E F A D V E R T I S E M E N T C O L U M N A K
N Y O G E E S Z H R H C B M Z M A S S M E D I A
T R B F Z U P Z E U E V O M A G P U B L I S H K
B Q J K F S R S P X U A Q N O C O V E R A G E A
R U E M W S I C R Z R Y M L F M A G A Z I N E A
A N C H O R N A E I J A B B K E I N F O R M E D
H F T W Z I T N S M P E D I T O R I A L S I E Y
L J I D P F M D S E X P O S E N J E W J U F M N
F Z V S X W E A H V E R I F Y E C E N S O R C I
L U E H E A D L I N E S R B L W W A T C H D O G
X R G M A N I P U L A T E O E S O U R C E S H V
A L T E R N A T I V E L F J G M H T A B L O I D
```

5·6 1. journalist 2. editorial 3. headline 4. objective 5. verify 6. magazine 7. blog 8. censor 9. front page 10. anchor 11. tabloids

Hidden message: Bad news travels fast.

6 Government and elections

6·1 1. candidate 2. political opponent 3. political party 4. campaign contributions 5. election campaign 6. smear campaign 7. platform 8. plank 9. endorsement 10. ballot 11. speech 12. incumbent 13. debate 14. poll 15. polling booth 16. exit poll 17. majority 18. landslide 19. coalition 20. dark horse

6·2 1. opposition party 2. voter turnout 3. coalition government 4. landslide victory 5. cast your vote 6. dark horse 7. run for government 8. smear campaign 9. party platform 10. free elections 11. exit polls 12. swing voter

6·3 **Candidates:** democratic, elections, candidates, party, independents, opponent, incumbent, reelected

Political parties: political, winning, platform, leader, toe, issue

Election campaigns: campaign, support, ads, speeches, debates, opponents, character, smear

Election day: booths, cast, counted, polls, turnout, recount

6·4 **Across:** 1. platform 6. swing 7. debate 9. vote 10. cast 11. poll 14. endorsement 16. turnout 17. toe 19. run 21. green 22. candidate

Down: 1. party 2. majority 3. contribution 4. landslide 5. independent 8. ballot 10. coalition 12. election 13. smear 15. campaign 18. opponent 20. speech

6·5

```
C A N D I D A T E E I N D E P E N D E N T E U N
E Z D R X Z P Y P W J D F E Y F I N I N U G E O
S T P C G S U A F B H S R N X D T P L I D I N Y
D E N D O R S E M E N T L B X N S J G W Z W R M
E V H N V A C C M W F F W D E M O C R A C Y O L
B Y X O E D O B O H V B O B V W H U D L H G E V
A U M O R U N Z I N V L M A E C M N A Y B I E F
T B O D N H T S M T S U S L T Z A C E P L T S N
E E S T M G R B X U C T G L O S I P B V Y Y G X
J L R Z E Q I S V N G I I O I T Y L N T N I T C
L H T I N J B V I P O L I T I C I A N D A V R A
M B W E T Q U G C A S T R L U T M N L P R R W G
A C O A L I T I O N U A O I D E P K M H T Y Z S
Y M A J O R I T Y U P P D R V X N A N Y Y B T L
O P L A T F O R M N C V O J J A C T E R F Z F U
R S M E A R N V O S O R O L Z E L E C T I O N N
G L O A K W P N P A R T Y T L A N D S L I D E U
D A R K H O R S E O C P Y U E O P P O N E N T Y
```

6·6 1. office 2. campaign 3. ballot 4. opponent 5. soapbox 6. dead 7. turnout 8. promise 9. dark 10. landslide 11. smear 12. hush 13. toe 14. stuff 15. towel 16. incorrect 17. swing 18. platform 19. renege

6·7 **Proverb 1:** Actions speak louder than words.

Proverb 2: Easier said than done.

7 Disease and medicine

7·1 1. germs, pathogens 2. immune system 3. specialist 4. antibiotics 5. vaccines 6. contagious 7. symptom 8. diagnosis 9. infection 10. epidemic 11. benign 12. patient 13. immunization 14. cure 15. relieve 16. chronic 17. lump, tumor 18. checkup

7·2 1. Types of infection 2. Cold symptoms 3. Skin ailments 4. Diagnosis aids 5. Remedies 6. Injuries 7. Contagious diseases 8. Medical professionals 9. Preventive measures

7·3 **A visit to the doctor:** health, general, symptoms, blood, diagnosis, treatment, prescription, specialist, opinion

The immune system: infections, viruses, parasites, medicine, tuberculosis, vaccinations, immune, eradicate

Cures and relief: purposes, cure, antibiotics, fungal, relieve, sore, bearable

Preventive measures: prevention, recovering, contracting, system, balanced, regular, vaccinations, hygiene, hand

7·4 **Across:** 2. vaccine 4. benign 5. chronic 6. immune 14. patient 15. contagious 16. opinion 17. painkiller 19. epidemic 21. parasite 23. surgery 25. pathogen 26. bacteria 27. germ 28. specialist

Down: 1. fungus 2. virus 3. ailment 5. checkup 7. symptom 8. infection 9. prescription 10. treatment 11. antibiotics 12. tumor 13. medicine 18. remedy 20. cure 22. recover 24. general

7·5

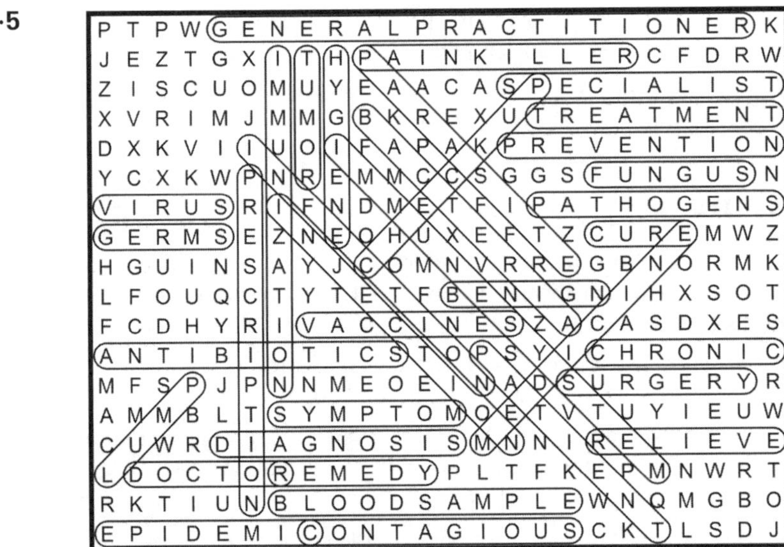

7·6 1. painkiller 2. virus 3. diagnosis 4. bruise 5. ailment 6. cut 7. symptom 8. chronic 9. surgery 10. cure 11. germs 12. infection

Hidden message: Laughter is the best medicine.

8 Psychology and mental disorders

8·1 1. abnormal 2. obsession 3. intuition 4. cope 5. disorder 6. abuse 7. aware 8. sensation 9. hallucination 10. suppress 11. self-esteem 12. mental 13. sociopath 14. delusion (possibly paranoia)

8·2 1. delusion 2. suppress 3. paranoid 4. sociopaths 5. obssessed 6. abused 7. amnesia 8. panic 9. empathy 10. hallucination 11. self-esteem 12. sensation

8·3 1. Instances of losing reality 2. Irrational fears or worries 3. Treatments for mental disorders 4. Words that mean "health problem" 5. Physical sensations 6. Ways to understand the world

8·4 **Mental disorders:** disorder, psychological, amnesia, insomnia, paranoia, panic, causes, social, discrimination

Déjà vu: sensation, been, done, déjà vu, French, eerie, recognize, surroundings

Hallucinations: hallucinations, real, mind, affect, crawling, common, voices, fever, dementia

Phobias: phobia, irrational, control, threat, terrified, confined, claustrophobia, fear, spiders

Clinical depression: blues, persistent, clinical, disorder, insomnia, disrupt, interest, antidepressant, counseling

8·5 1. blow 2. lose 3. make 4. eye 5. ease 6. right 7. out 8. absent-minded 9. lot 10. positive 11. take 12. slipped 13. read 14. keep 15. mind-boggling 16. speak 17. crossed 18. blank

8·6 look like you've seen a ghost

8·7 1. phobia 2. insomnia 3. amnesia 4. anxiety 5. cope 6. sensation 7. obsession 8. paranoia 9. nightmare 10. disorder 11. sociopath

Hidden message: Great minds think alike.

8·8 1. nightmare 2. daydream 3. empathy 4. mental 5. phobia 6. denial 7. disorder 8. cope 9. paranoia 10. abuse 11. amnesia 12. anxiety 13. suppress 14. sensation 15. abnormal

8·9 **Idiom 1:** lose your marbles

Idiom 2: come to your senses

8·10 **Across:** 2. mental 5. irrational 7. denial 8. phobia 10. panic 14. paranoia 15. hallucination 18. intuition 19. self-esteem 20. empathy

Down: 1. perception 3. aware 4. sensation 6. disorder 7. depression 9. unconscious 11. amnesia 12. insomnia 13. obsession 16. abuse 17. anxiety

9 Problems and solutions

9·1 1. deteriorate 2. futile 3. obstacle, impediment, stumbling block 4. prudent 5. dilemma 6. impact 7. sustainable 8. feasible 9. brainstorm 10. avert 11. last resort, extreme measures 12. panacea 13. fortify 14. scapegoat

9·2 1. minor setback 2. last resort 3. worst-case scenario 4. extreme measures 5. stumbling block 6. cost effective 7. underlying cause 8. beyond hope

9·3 1. Things that get in the way 2. Prevent from doing 3. Make less severe 4. Problem situations 5. Criteria for evaluating solutions 6. What is done when all else fails 7. Solutions 8. Fundamental reasons a problem occurs 9. Can't be solved

9·4 **Dilemmas:** dilemma, undesirable, evils, Odysseus, sea monsters, opted, risk, consequences

Indentifying problems: crisis, underlying, solutions, gather, interviewing, experts, case, multiple, biased

Coming up with solutions: brainstorm, potential, ideas, matter, evaluate, mistake, mind, outside, perspective

Evaluating solutions: come, criteria, paper, feasible, consider, effective, effort, sustainable, temporary

Extreme measures: insurmountable, measures, fails, last, desperate, risky, morally, question, justifies

9·5 1. brainstorm 2. adversity 3. dilemma 4. gamble 5. solution 6. lesser 7. devise 8. gather 9. perspective 10. mitigate 11. measures 12. worst-case 13. cause 14. resort 15. costs 16. situation 17. block 18. hope

9·6 There is more than one way to skin a cat.

9·7 1. predicament 2. obstacle 3. futile 4. prevail 5. scapegoat 6. deteriorate 7. dilemma 8. panacea 9. measures 10. crisis 11. lesser 12. impact

Hidden message: dig your own grave

9·8 1. solution 2. dilemma 3. obstacle 4. strengthen 5. crisis 6. prevail 7. hinder 8. feasible 9. brainstorm 10. last resort 11. panacea 12. impact 13. predicament 14. scapegoat 15. worsen 16. drawback

9·9 caught between a rock and a hard place

9·10 **Across:** 2. beyond 5. panacea 8. birds 10. solution 11. resort 13. deteriorate 14. devil 15. dilemma 17. measures 19. feasible 20. rock 22. obstacle 24. predicament 26. root

Down: 1. grave 2. brainstorm 3. futile 4. hinder 6. evils 7. mitigate 9. solve 12. outside 16. impact 18. extreme 21. cost 23. come 25. cat

10 Technology and innovation

10·1 1. trademark 2. copyright 3. patent 4. obsolete 5. component 6. modify 7. gadget 8. entrepreneur 9. hybrid 10. groundbreaking, visionary, original, novel, cutting-edge, state-of-the-art 11. conceive 12. augment 13. visionary 14. foster, inspire 15. unique novel, original 16. novel, original

10·2 1. intellectual property rights 2. technological breakthrough 3. product life cycle 4. advances in technology 5. computer literate 6. added features 7. bells and whistles 8. digital cameras

10·3 1. Words that mean "create" 2. Adjectives used to describe advanced technologies 3. Machines or tools 4. Intellectual property rights 5. Words that mean "change" 6. New technologies 7. People involved in developing new technologies 8. Words used to describe old technologies 9. Parts of something

10·4 **Technology:** history, technologies, revolutionized, vaccinations, life span, process, agricultural, printing, information

Technology and the product life cycle: consumer, art, prices, products, down, edge, replaced, obsolete, cycle

Modifying old technologies: innovations, existing, modified, augmenting, features, access, materials, lightweight, performance

Drawbacks of technology: widespread, drawbacks, detrimental, point, durable, materials, pesticides, deforming

Intellectual property rights: rewarded, intellectual, incentive, exclusive, patent, invention, period, copyright

10·5 1. program 2. online 3. improved 4. delete 5. features 6. ideas 7. ahead 8. savvy 9. literate 10. information 11. engine 12. access 13. bells 14. connection 15. device 16. rocket 17. tech 18. Web

10·6 **Idiom 1:** go back to the drawing board

Idiom 2: start from scratch

10·7 1. invention 2. cutting-edge 3. innovation 4. prototype 5. patent 6. hybrid 7. obsolete 8. component 9. modify 10. device 11. copyright

Hidden message: reinvent the wheel

10·8 **Across:** 1. develop 5. design 6. hybrid 7. delete 8. augment 9. access 11. conceive 14. wireless 15. install 17. novel 18. invention 20. copyright 22. patent 23. feature

Down: 1. device 2. obsolete 3. intellectual 4. innovation 10. creativity 12. component 13. improved 16. prototype 19. edge 21. art

10·9 1. innovation 2. device 3. gadget 4. create 5. patent 6. obsolete 7. prototype 8. component 9. feature 10. conceive 11. modify 12. hybrid 13. high tech 14. novel 15. inspiration 16. design

10·10 Necessity is the mother of invention.

11 History and civilization

11·1 1. agriculture 2. irrigation 3. arable 4. oral tradition 5. nomad 6. clan 7. archeology 8. architecture 9. barter 10. settlement 11. mythology 12. navigation 13. domestication 14. monument

11·2 1. Metallurgy 2. People who study the past 3. Ancient civilizations 4. Systems of writing 5. Locations of ancient civilizations 6. Prehistoric periods 7. Monumental architecture 8. Organized religion 9. Social stratification

11·3 **Historical people:** aristocrat, explorer, scribe, slave, artisan, emperor, peasant, monk

Historical eras: Industrial Revolution, Age of Exploration, Middle Ages, Iron Age, Renaissance, Bronze Age, Reformation, Enlightenment

11·4 **Early peoples:** ancestors, gatherers, nomadic, clans, writing, bone, archeologists, artifacts

Agriculture: civilization, valleys, agriculture, settle, irrigation, ditches, floods, fertile, surplus

Hierarchical societies: spread, artisans, pottery, hierarchical, privileges, chiefs, status, aristocrats, slavery

Early technologies: characteristics, technology, ability, ward, significance, bone, skins, survive, migration

The development of writing: achievements, generation, spoken, tradition, literacy, scribes, printing, affordable

11·5 1. Renaissance 2. Great Depression 3. Enlightenment 4. industrial revolution 5. First World War 6. Gold Rush 7. Bronze Age 8. Cold War 9. American Civil War 10. Black Death 11. French Revolution 12. Age of Exploration 13. Middle Ages

Clue 1: Achilles' heel

Clue 2: Midas touch

Clue 3: Pandora's box

11·6 1. archeologist 2. barter 3. artifact 4. nomad 5. slave 6. artisan 7. dynasty 8. ruins 9. surplus 10. agriculture 11. circa 12. mythology

Hidden message: a Spartan existence

11·7 **Across:** 2. conquer 6. ruins 8. artifact 9. writing 10. artisan 13. irrigation 14. domestication 16. nomad 19. surplus 21. bronze 22. literacy

Down: 1. archeologist 2. circa 3. oral 4. civilization 5. navigation 7. scribe 10. agriculture 11. trade 12. remains 15. barter 17. myth 18. dynasty 20. slave

11·8 1. mythology 2. barter 3. ruins 4. agriculture 5. civilization 6. artifact 7. ancestor 8. circa 9. irrigation 10. dynasty 11. age 12. bronze 13. monuments 14. write 15. surplus

11·9 **Proverb 1:** Rome wasn't built in a day.

Proverb 2: History repeats itself.

12 Banking and personal finance

12·1 1. deposit 2. withdraw 3. transaction 4. debt 5. balance 6. statement 7. mortgage 8. interest 9. assets 10. insurance 11. teller 12. pension 13. funds 14. cash 15. investment 16. stocks 17. bonds 18. risk 19. checking 20. savings

12·2 1. stocks 2. return 3. insurance 4. transaction 5. diversify 6. housing

12·3 **Bank accounts:** sums, robbed, fire, deposit, savings, checking, interest, transaction, debit, withdraw

Buying a house: purchase, afford, funds, mortgage, payment, percent, credit, market, estate

Investing your money: safest, rate, return, risk, invest, stocks, profit, bonds, bankrupt

12·4 1. go bankrupt 2. default on a loan 3. interest rate 4. real estate 5. debit card 6. invest in stocks

12·5 **Across:** 2. bills 6. return 7. cash 8. withdraw 10. teller 11. debit 14. loan 20. fee 21. funds 22. investor 26. transaction 29. estate 30. debt 31. insurance

Down: 1. deposit 2. bankrupt 3. stocks 4. statement 5. budget 9. diversify 12. investment 13. payment 15. credit 16. interest 17. default 18. risk 19. mortgage 23. pension 24. balance 25. asset 27. coins 28. bonds

12·6

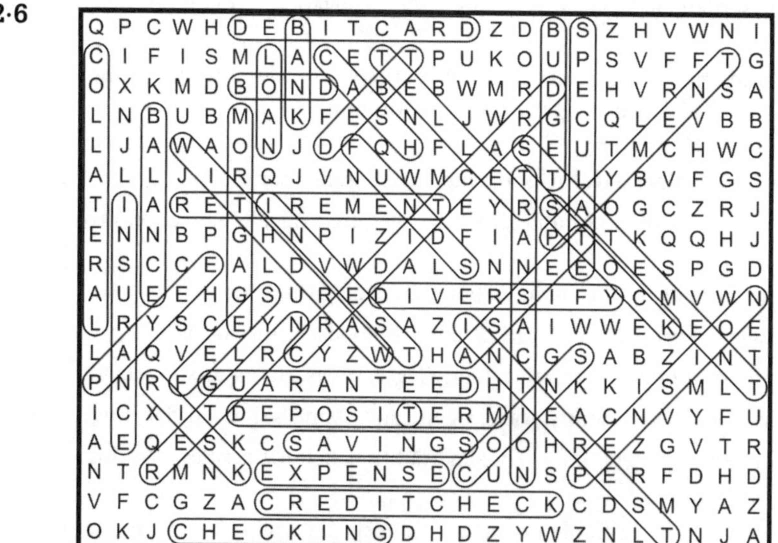

12·7 1. penny 2. budget 3. broke 4. bill 5. burn 6. save 7. dime 8. riches 9. goldmine 10. rainy 11. meet 12. cheap 13. squirrel 14. shirt 15. touch 16. robbery 17. feed 18. beware 19. belt

12·8 Money is the root of all evil.

13 The economy

13·1 1. corporation 2. currency 3. surplus 4. scarcity 5. central bank 6. regulate 7. asset 8. monopoly 9. free enterprise 10. capital 11. consumer 12. producer 13. bailout 14. supply 15. demand 16. exchange rate 17. GDP 18. economic indicators

13·2 1. Economic downturns 2. Market forces 3. Services 4. Goods 5. Human resources 6. International trade

13·3 1. central 2. real 3. per 4. goods 5. raw 6. free 7. supply 8. human 9. tariff 10. balance 11. division 12. market 13. exchange 14. stock 15. trade

13·4 **Goods and services:** market, goods, touch, tangible, transported, owner, service, cut, teach, intangible

Consumers and producers: consumers, purchase, producers, bakery, factories, capital, raw, human

Market forces: forces, supply, demand, surplus, drop, scarcity, rise, monopoly

International trade: exchange, import, export, balance, impose, tariffs, trade, free

13·5

13·6 **Across:** 4. outsource 5. asset 7. finished 9. income 10. raw 11. import 12. debt 14. scarcity 16. loan 17. market 19. inflation 20. free 23. supply 24. recession 25. strike 27. human 28. unemployment 29. enterprise 31. union 32. currency

Down: 1. loss 2. balance 3. bailout 6. tariff 7. forces 8. export 12. demand 13. capital 15. interest 18. profit 21. exchange 22. consumer 23. surplus 26. monopoly 30. tax

13·7 1. inflation 2. consumer 3. recession 4. service 5. exports 6. imports 7. interest 8. supply 9. demand 10. currency 11. market 12. GDP 13. trade

Hidden message: a booming economy

13·8 1. even 2. stock 3. corners 4. figure 5. bang 6. red 7. black 8. supply 9. rally 10. roll out 11. belly 12. shop 13. risk 14. mouth 15. goods 16. hotcakes 17. bargaining 18. works 19. market

13·9 **Proverb 1:** Look before you leap.

Proverb 2: Opportunity only knocks once.

14 Life science

14·1 1. flora 2. fauna 3. herbivore 4. carnivore 5. trait 6. heredity 7. organism 8. predator 9. prey 10. vertebrate 11. classification 12. habitat 13. cell 14. adaptation

14·2 1. recessive 2. food 3. sexual 4. survival 5. life 6. symbiotic 7. predator 8. natural

14·3 1. vertebrates 2. mammals 3. primates 4. hominids 5. humans

14·4 1. Physical/structural adaptations 2. Relations in a food web 3. Vertebrates 4. Plant reproduction 5. Behavioral adaptations 6. Insect life cycle 7. Theory of evolution 8. Heredity 9. Relationships between organisms

14·5 **Reptile:** snake, turtle, lizard

Mammal: gorilla, horse, whale

Mollusk: clam, octopus, snail

Crustacean: crab, shrimp, lobster

Amphibian: frog, toad, salamander

14·6 **Characteristics of living organisms:** organisms, characteristics, cells, energy, grow, stimuli, environment, reproduce

Animal classification: biologists, sort, traits, classified, invertebrates, reptiles, mammals, hand, crustaceans

The theory of evolution: published, selection, claimed, environment, reproduce, adaptation, generation, survival

The principles of heredity: trait, offspring, pass, heredity, genes, inherited, recessive, both

Relations in a food web: web, predator, eaten, apex, balance, population, grazing, vegetation

14·7 1. snake 2. worms 3. squirrel 4. flies 5. share 6. pace 7. hornet's nest 8. bat 9. pants 10. monkey 11. dogs 12. fry 13. clam 14. crow 15. wolf 16. deer 17. bull 18. rat

14·8 The apple doesn't fall far from the tree.

14·9 1. mutation 2. amphibian 3. instinct 4. organism 5. reptile 6. prey 7. trait 8. heredity 9. cell 10. vertebrate 11. flora 12. omnivore 13. primate

Hidden message: a dog-eat-dog world

14·10 **Across:** 1. parasite 6. fauna 8. adaptation 9. habitat 11. vertebrate 12. symbiosis 15. gene 16. reptile 18. omnivore 21. organism 22. heredity

Down: 1. predator 2. trait 3. carnivore 4. offspring 5. food web 7. flora 9. herbivore 10. instinct 12. species 13. cell 14. mutation 17. primate 19. mammal 20. prey

14·11 1. predator 2. herbivore 3. vertebrate 4. parasite 5. trait 6. habitat 7. organism 8. reptile 9. primate 10. species 11. offspring 12. gene 13. evolution 14. mutation 15. heredity

14·12 the bottom of the food chain

15 The environment: Issues and conservation

15·1 1. global warming 2. climate change 3. invasive species 4. overfishing 5. disposable 6. landfill 7. roadkill 8. urban sprawl 9. pesticide 10. detergent 11. deforestation 12. desertification 13. carbon dioxide 14. acid rain 15. exhaust fumes 16. endangered species 17. extinct 18. polar ice cap 19. habitat loss 20. whaling 21. ozone layer 22. greenhouse effect

15·2 1. fossil 2. habitat 3. endangered 4. invasive 5. greenhouse 6. bush 7. acid 8. disposable 9. global 10. oil 11. toxic 12. exhaust 13. climate 14. urban 15. ozone

15·3 1. Causes of extinction 2. Environmental disasters 3. Extinct species 4. Endangered species 5. Fossil fuels 6. Atmospheric gases 7. Examples of climate change 8. Threatened habitats 9. Sources of air pollution

15·4 **Environmental pollution:** environmental, fumes, smog, detergents, fertilizers, toxic, leaks, contaminates, plastic

Global warming and climate change: climate, gases, global, greenhouse, dioxide, temperature, sea, fossil, livestock

Habitat loss: hunting, bush, loss, deforestation, clear, lumber, extinct, wetlands, nesting, change

Decreasing biodiversity: living, ecosystem, species, web, predators, insects, balance, habitat, invasive

15·5

L	Y	C	G	R	E	E	N	B	E	L	T	E	D	E	T	E	R	G	E	N	T	N	A
F	A	O	E	A	Z	V	F	E	C	O	S	Y	S	T	E	M	C	E	T	J	Z	B	C
O	M	N	N	I	Y	F	A	X	U	U	Y	C	I	P	R	O	T	E	C	T	E	D	H
S	P	T	D	N	B	I	O	D	E	G	R	A	D	A	B	L	E	E	W	Y	Q	R	V
S	O	A	A	F	S	O	P	R	C	P	E	S	T	I	C	I	D	E	L	Y	C	Y	H
I	A	M	N	O	I	I	O	P	E	O	E	T	O	X	I	C	W	A	S	T	E	L	V
L	C	I	G	R	N	L	L	C	A	R	B	O	N	F	O	O	T	P	R	I	N	T	E
F	H	N	E	E	V	S	L	M	V	G	L	O	B	A	L	W	A	R	M	I	N	G	T
U	I	A	R	S	A	P	U	W	H	A	L	I	N	G	W	I	L	D	L	I	F	E	Z
E	N	T	E	T	S	I	T	U	Z	N	X	H	A	B	I	T	A	T	L	O	S	S	E
L	G	I	D	R	I	L	I	I	A	I	J	X	U	O	Z	O	N	E	L	A	Y	E	R
E	K	O	F	U	V	L	O	Y	G	C	C	O	N	S	E	R	V	A	T	I	O	N	F
X	E	N	G	R	E	E	N	H	O	U	S	E	E	F	F	E	C	T	F	H	Z	M	Z
T	I	A	V	C	U	C	A	R	B	O	N	D	I	O	X	I	D	E	A	J	N	A	W
I	R	E	D	U	C	E	D	E	S	E	R	T	I	F	I	C	A	T	I	O	N	U	F
N	D	I	S	P	O	S	A	B	L	E	L	R	W	K	E	X	H	A	U	S	T	U	D
C	U	S	O	L	A	R	E	N	E	R	G	Y	A	C	I	D	R	A	I	N	P	H	W
T	A	G	E	M	C	O	N	S	U	M	P	T	I	O	N	Q	C	O	M	P	O	S	T

15·6 **Across:** 5. urban 7. carbon 8. exhaust 9. acid 10. spill 12. deforestation 13. extinct 16. endangered 20. plastic 22. fossil 23. overfishing 24. whaling

Down: 1. habitat 2. landfill 3. fertilizer 4. greenhouse 6. pollution 10. smog 11. pesticide 14. toxic 15. invasive 17. roadkill 18. detergent 19. ozone 21. global

15·7 1. consumption 2. reduce 3. reuse 4. recycle 5. carbon footprint 6. compost 7. solar energy 8. hydroelectric energy 9. organic 10. poaching 11. protected species 12. biodiversity 13. nature reserve 14. sustainable development 15. greenbelt 16. energy efficient 17. biodegradable 18. public transportation 19. wildlife 20. conservation

15·8 1. Ways to reduce litter 2. Eco-friendly product labels 3. Alternative energy sources 4. Ways to conserve biodiversity 5. Things that waste resources 6. Ways to conserve fossil fuels

15·9 **Reducing waste:** environmental, ocean, landfills, reduce, disposable, purchasing, cloth, recycle, glass

Reducing your carbon footprint: warming, carbon, greenhouse, measure, consumption, livestock, emissions, fuels, public

Protecting endangered species: endangered, biodiversity, passed, threat, poachers, ivory, ban, black, enforced

Using alternative energy sources: fossil, resources, linked, reliance, alternative, wind, power, renewable

15·10 **Across:** 2. consumption 6. fossil 8. reuse 9. leaky 12. car 13. heat 14. down 16. biodegradable 18. footprint 20. disposable 21. biodiversity 22. conserve

Down: 1. eco-friendly 3. solar 4. poaching 5. recycle 7. sustainable 10. detergent 11. reduce 12. compost 15. alternative 17. efficient 19. public

16 Human rights

16·1 1. fundamental 2. freedom, liberty 3. equality 4. universal 5. inalienable 6. due process 7. impartial 8. gender 9. ethnicity 10. religion 11. abolition 12. discrimination, prejudice 13. deprive, deny 14. segregation 15. violation 16. torture 17. thought 18. genocide 19. atrocities 20. human rights

16·2 **Basic principles of human rights:** rights, violation, equality, discriminate, gender, principle, inalienable, torturing

Universal suffrage and the suffragettes: vote, universal, deprived, women, property, population, discrimination, demand, suffragettes

Universal declaration of human rights: atrocities, rights, slave, genocide, minorities, fundamental, race, Declaration

Crimes against humanity: abuses, humanity, classified, isolated, genocide, destruction, torture

16·3 **Across:** 1. genocide 3. deprive 6. slavery 10. universal 11. process 12. speech 16. freedom 19. torture 20. discrimination 21. ethnicity

Down: 1. gender 2. inalienable 4. impartial 5. religion 6. suffrage 7. liberty 8. fundamental 9. persecution 13. prejudice 14. human rights 15. equality 17. abolition 18. violation

16·4

```
S E L F D E T E R M I N A T I O N M R N S F B M
W Y W U Z W A H W J U S T I C E Q U A L I T Y P
J D S Y Z O L X T S P H H U N I V E R S A L A N
W W E J G U X I Y W W G X O S R V G T N N L O E
J V A T R O C I T I E S A E M L F W O J N I D D
D C U C H C G E N D E R S N K H I I J A S I R T
S E G R E G A T I O N U O V R Z T B E S C B E Q
D V I O L A T I O N B I V C P A W R E O B F C L
T U M M P Z R E H A T N Q C N U U R N R W G J L
H A E Y P V G S G U W A G I X T P E K V T E O N
O O D P B A M L C M T L M M R X G E P S R Y H G
U R S E R O R E Q Y W I X O E A B O L I T I O N
G F X F D O S T N Y R E T H N I C I T Y S B G B
H J F E B R C E I C U N N Y D E P R I V E W O K
T U E I E P D E S A W A M I N O R I T I E S U V
S R L P N C O I S V L B P R E J U D I C E J R C
F I I S Y L D K K S D L K H U M A N R I G H T S
F U N D A M E N T A L E R E L I G I O N B Y D O
```

17 International relations

17·1 1. treaty 2. alliance 3. cooperation 4. capital 5. government 6. NGO 7. nation-state 8. diplomat 9. ambassador 10. embassy 11. multinational 12. national interest 13. negotiations 14. arms race 15. sanctions 16. deterrence 17. reciprocity 18. sovereignty 19. border 20. imperialism

17·2 1. nongovernmental 2. cultural 3. humanitarian 4. arms 5. diplomatic 6. arms 7. trade 8. nation 9. regional 10. balance 11. the United 12. multinational

17·3 **Diplomatic relations:** negotiations, conflict, resolution, interests, benefit, mission, ambassador, diplomat, embassy

International cooperation: cooperate, mutual, barriers, resources, whaling, greenhouse, reciprocity, receives

International organizations: organization, Borders, nonprofit, independent, multinational, profits, sovereign, United

Balance of power: balance, dominate, combine, collective, hegemon, alliances, deter, World

17·4 **Across:** 4. embassy 5. deter 10. sanctions 11. alliance 12. border 14. sovereignty 17. cooperate 19. reciprocity 20. United 21. arms 22. multinational 23. domestic 24. treaty

Down: 1. interest 2. foreign 3. collective 4. embargo 5. diplomacy 6. ambassador 7. capital 8. diplomat 9. balance 13. negotiations 15. imperialism 16. government 18. mutual

17·5

A C O L L E C T I V E S E C U R I T Y O Z T X C
R F P P M G X Q U O J A M B A S S A D O R J B S
M H M U L T I N A T I O N A L N W W Z E M W J I
S O V E R E I G N T Y U F G O G C J J Q Z W I O
C X U S H U M A N I T A R I A N D I P L O M A T
O X T Q B O R D E R E D T D I S A R M A M E N T
N G F W O F N Y X C P A R E G I O N A L B L O C
T E J C A P I T A L N E G O T I A T I O N S E L
R H A Y Y G A R I D F H N A T I O N S T A T E B
O S B L I P S E E L U F K U E M B A S S Y R U X
L A T B L M F T R A D E T E R R E N C E F U W P
E N I N R I I M P E R I A L I S M T R E A T Y D
M C E A F N A T I O N A L I N T E R E S T J D E
B T G X U B G N N G L O B A L I Z A T I O N U D
A I T M L F T O C B V F O R E I G N P O L I C Y
R O G O V E R N M E N T R E C I P R O C I T Y D
G N I R I D Z E C O O P E R A T I O N O E P G S
O S D O M E S T I C P O L I C Y H E G E M O N Z

17·6 1. trade 2. treaty 3. allies 4. arms race 5. ambassador 6. embargo 7. border 8. disarmament 9. cooperation 10. nation 11. foreign

Hidden message: gunboat diplomacy

18 Human conflict

18·1 1. conflict 2. civil war 3. belligerent 4. front line 5. siege 6. casualties 7. refugees 8. death toll 9. collateral damage 10. espionage 11. infantry 12. drone 13. artillery 14. minefield 15. crisis 16. border dispute 17. combatant 18. peace treaty 19. guerrillas 20. rebels 21. surrender 22. navy 23. truce 24. Geneva conventions

18·2 1. Cessation of hostilities 2. Types of attack 3. Munitions 4. Noncombatants 5. Casualties 6. Branches of the military

18·3 **Arms control:** destructiveness, munitions, children, civilians, poison, biological, land mines, maiming

Words used to describe conflict: describe, siege, raid, ambush, preemptive, espionage, sabotage, blockade

Geneva conventions: treaties, limit, civilians, prisoners, wounded, torture, treatment, property

Cessation of hostilities: Armistice, cessation, ceasefire, relief, combatants, optimism, toll, trench, chemical

18·4 **Across:** 2. peace 4. front 9. collateral 10. armistice 12. navy 14. preemptive 15. civil 16. guerrillas 20. armor 22. ambush 24. munitions 25. blockade 26. refugee 27. belligerent

Down: 1. infantry 3. combatant 5. toll 6. air force 7. peacekeepers 8. land mine 10. artillery 11. siege 13. raid 15. casualty 17. surrender 18. espionage 19. sabotage 21. prisoner 23. drone

18·5

L A N D M I N E W O U N D E D B A L L I A N C E
Q L A O P S U R R E N D E R I C O N F L I C T S
T R U C E G U E R R I L L A S V Y M R N E K E W
Y P D I A C Y B D T N S Y E R M G I B V T N J Y
L R O S C O V E Z P E W E A R Z L S I E I S H W
A A D D E L H L C G N G W A Z Q N T E R R A P Y
R U O E K D M S E R U L E M R O P R A S A G Q M
M S A V E W K I L F X N W G I M I M E Q Q E S H
I Q I A E A S F E V I S L T E F O I Y N D E X I
S C R S P R P R I L X L I E E N T R A A I E Z J
T O F T I M C C T S O N R S G I E I K T G E Z D
I M O A N O Q N P T U P A A L L L C L A L M A D
C B R T G Y O O H M Z E V I L I O A N I Z S R E
E A C I Q R O T I W C A T I V L U O S E A B U M
N T E O F R A G P O P S T I B S I S O Z E C Z K
A A A N T E L K O Y O R C D A P I E T R D G O P
V N I N D R O N E H A I H C S M D I S P U T E F
Y T W K K T P Q E N S A B E R R A T T L I N G O

19 Describing materials and objects

19·1 1. audible 2. fragile, brittle, flimsy 3. transparent 4. massive, colossal 5. corrossive 6. hollow 7. tangible 8. versatile 9. lethal, toxic, hazardous 10. microscopic, miniature, miniscule 11. symmetrical 12. harmless 13. flexible 14. portable

19·2 **Positive:** portable, sturdy, lightweight, durable

Negative: bulky, toxic, flimsy, brittle

19·3 1. Large 2. Small 3. Not clear 4. Rough textures 5. Easy to break 6. Potentially harmful 7. Easy to bend or stretch 8. Not easy to bend or stretch 9. Clear

19·4 **Transparent materials:** light, through, transmits, transparent, glasses, opaque, shadows, murky, filter

Hazardous materials: health, corrosive, noxious, lethal, regulations, transported, dispose, chemicals, contaminating

Portable goods: portable, producers, size, lightweight, compact, bulky, durable

Plastic: plastic, versatile, pliable, mold, sturdy, waterproof, containers, shatter, lightweight

19·5 1. glass 2. plastic 3. gold 4. silk 5. copper 6. wood 7. rubber 8. diamond 9. steel 10. mercury 11. acid 12. cardboard 13. aluminum

Simile 1: as cold as ice

Simile 2: as black as coal

Simile 3: as slippery as an eel

19·6 1. versatile 2. harmless 3. massive 4. hard 5. sharp 6. brittle 7. miniature 8. miniscule 9. flexible 10. sturdy 11. toxic 12. hollow 13. cloudy 14. audible 15. visible

Hidden message: as clear as mud

19·7 1. bulky 2. toxic 3. portable 4. lethal 5. transparent 6. fragile 7. visible 8. massive 9. tangible 10. rigid 11. durable 12. versatile 13. opaque 14. hollow 15. corrosive

19·8 The tree that doesn't bend breaks.

19·9 **Across:** 5. audible 6. elastic 8. rigid 11. versatile 14. murky 15. dull 17. hollow 19. transparent 22. microscopic 24. lethal 26. miniscule

Down: 1. massive 2. coarse 3. fragile 4. bulky 7. flimsy 9. durable 10. hazardous 12. colossal 13. smooth 16. corrosive 18. harmless 20. portable 21. visible 23. opaque 25. toxic

20 Demographic trends

20·1 1. household 2. nuclear family 3. extended family 4. single-parent household 5. literacy rate 6. industrialization 7. middle class 8. unemployment rate 9. debt burden 10. materialism 11. infant mortality rate 12. life expectancy 13. population 14. urbanization 15. standard of living 16. quality of life 17. early retirement 18. environmental awareness 19. divorce rate 20. cost of living 21. inflation 22. poverty line 23. birth rate

20·2 **Upward trends:** going up, increasing, on the rise, rising, growing, soaring, skyrocketing, surging

Steady trends: leveled off, unchanged, stable, steady, plateaued, bottomed out

Downward trends: declining, on the decline, decreasing, falling, shrinking, plummeting, slipping, going down, sinking, dropping

20·3 **The standard of living:** standard, economies, consumer, middle, developed, dramatically, poverty

Life expectancy: material, substantial, expectancy, mortality, dropped, sanitation, spread, treatments

Population: population, age, case, decline, rate, money, rapidly

Education: public, compulsory, literacy, skyrocketed, skilled, productive, masses

A sustainable lifestyle: debate, adverse, climate, fossil, run, technologies, solve

20·4 1. comedian 2. armor 3. donate 4. acorn 5. caption 6. archer 7. chain 8. diamond 9. garden 10. cinema 11. gather 12. cheater 13. compare 14. cargo 15. admire 16. code 17. depart 18. anchor 19. dragon 20. chore 21. champion 22. erode 23. crate 24. coin 25. agree 26. Earth 27. diet 28. hidden

20·5 **Major/large change:** considerable, dramatic, sharp, significant, substantial, sudden

Steady change: consistent, gradual, steady

Minor/insignificant change: insignificant, marginal, modest, negligible, slight

20·6 1. increase gradually 2. drop suddenly 3. decrease sharply 4. rise dramatically 5. decline marginally 6. rise steadily 7. grow modestly 8. drop consistently

20·7 **Across:** 1. middle 3. public 5. cost 8. poverty 9. birth 12. extended 16. industrialization 21. unemployment 23. migration 24. expectancy

Down: 2. decline 4. living 6. skyrocket 7. urbanization 8. population 10. household 11. mortality 13. nuclear 14. rise 15. literacy 16. inflation 17. divorce 18. quality 19. plummet 20. single 22. level

20·8 1. life 2. average 3. single 4. debt 5. birth 6. bottomed 7. dramatic 8. standard 9. leveled 10. middle 11. nuclear 12. poverty

20·9

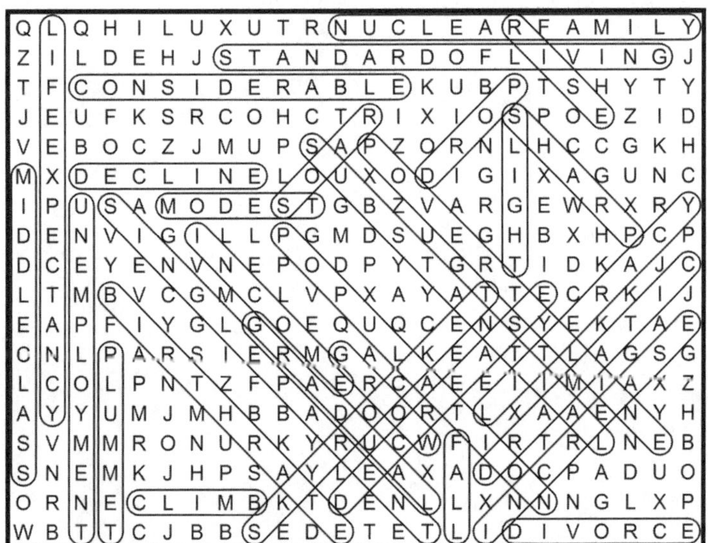

21 Theory and research

21·1 1. disprove, refute, debunk 2. plausible 3. dubious 4. paradox 5. phenomena 6. misconception, fallacy 7. debate 8. enigma, paradox 9. hypothesis, conjecture 10. speculate, extrapolate 11. paradigm 12. extrapolate, speculate 13. empirical 14. sample size

21·2 1. causal 2. empirical 3. design 4. scientific 5. common 6. peer 7. formulate 8. paradigm

21·3 1. How phenomena are connected 2. Empirical evidence 3. Natural phenomena 4. Mistaken beliefs 5. The scientific method 6. State that something is true 7. Doubtful 8. Possibly true 9. Speculate

21·4 1. empirical 2. disprove 3. plausible 4. contradict 5. anomaly 6. correlation 7. speculate 8. ambiguous 9. scrutinize 10. conjecture 11. enigma 12. extrapolate

21·5 1. cause 2. correlation 3. sample 4. method 5. shift 6. peer 7. hypothesis 8. empirical 9. misconception 10. journal 11. phenomena 12. contradiction 13. evidence 14. observation 15. point 16. experiment 17. record 18. disprove

21·6 **Idiom 1:** hit the nail on the head

Idiom 2: jump to conclusions

21·7 **The scientific method:** method, phenomena, hypotheses, experiments, empirical, observation, peer, verified, reproduce

Paradigm shifts: model, modified, observations, history, revolution, shift, anomaly, explained

Cause and effect versus correlation: coincidence, correlation, fallacy, causes, statistical, necessarily, case, depends

Paradoxes: paradox, puzzles, critical, assume, conclude, contradiction, other, according, replaced

21·8 1. extrapolate 2. empirical 3. fallacy 4. phenomena 5. paradox 6. data 7. hypothesis 8. speculate 9. assert 10. refute 11. proof

Hidden message: put two and two together

21·9 **Across:** 1. conjecture 4. peer 7. data 9. anomaly 10. plausible 11. misconception 15. shift 17. proof 19. ambiguous 23. extrapolate 24. scrutinize 25. phenomena

Down: 2. contradict 3. dubious 4. paradox 5. assert 6. claim 8. debate 12. empirical 13. hypothesis 14. speculate 16. absurd 18. fallacy 20. paradigm 21. method 22. refute

21·10 1. anomaly 2. assert 3. paradigm 4. enigma 5. proof 6. fallacy 7. disprove 8. paradox 9. dubious 10. hypothesis 11. phenomena 12. data 13. experiment 14. peer 15. debunk

21·11 The facts speak for themselves.